THE DEVOTED CALL FOR HOPE

MUSTAFA, THE SON OF SULTAN SULEIMAN

Novel by

Ridvan Akbay

Contact the author at ridvanakbay@icloud.com

Published by Ben Oak Publishing

ISBN
Paperbook: ISBN-13: 979-8714588921
ebook: ASIN: B08XP4YXS8
audiobook: ASIN: B0933JWQ9F

First Edition.

Edited, formatted, proofread, and cover designed by the publisher.

CONTENTS

DEDICATED TO

Dedicated to Ahmet, thank you for being here.

DISCLAIMER

Although the sentence-layer and the publisher have made every reasonable effort to ensure that the information in this book was correct at the time of publishing, both the sentence-layer and the publisher do not assume, and hereby disclaim any liability to any party for any loss, damage, or disruption caused by errors or omissions, whether such errors or omissions result from negligence, accident, or any other cause.

PREFACE

*Spite everything and the enemy, we will live. Tomorrow is ours." ---
Yilmaz Guney*

Three questions to answer, before diving into the story of Prince Mustafa, as it will be on the readers' minds. Furthermore, let us erase any misconceptions and fallacies that the readers might have, and only focus on the intriguing story and not the sentence-layer.

The three questions were chosen by the sentence-layer, and he has predicted that it will be the same questions or similar questions on the readers' minds, and as explained above, it is best to answer the questions, before starting the story.

The three important and relevant questions were chosen to be answered are:
1. Who are you?
2. Why are you writing this story?
3. Will we learn anything more about Prince Mustafa, which we have not already known about previously?

Who are you?

My name is *Ridvan Akbay*, call me Rid or the Riddler. I have lived the majority of my life in Canada, outside of my birthplace of Istanbul, Turkey. I have lived in the west, the home of the free, where I witnessed many interesting and thought-provoking processes, while advancing through the educational system, which I would like to focus on and share. Furthermore, comparing the educational system between the two countries will be helpful and advantageous to answer the question, *who are you,* properly.

My educational background is very fascinating, to say the least, and it would be best to elaborate on this now.

My first three grades at elementary school were completed in Turkey, but since we immigrated to Canada, I finished elementary school in our new country. Then, we moved back to Turkey temporarily, and I finished junior high school there. Again we moved, and I started grade 10 in Canada and finished high school here. My college diploma and university degree are from Canada. Therefore, as evidenced, I have a diversified and noteworthy educational background. It is striking in that we got to see many different schools and saw the curriculum change frequently.

In Turkey, while attending school, among the usual subjects such as Math, Turkish writing and reading, English as a second language, Chemistry, Biology, Physics, we also learned History, which by the way happened to be my favorite subject. Particularly, the topics of *History of the Republic of Turkey*, *Founder of the Republic - Mustafa Kemal Ataturk*, and the *Ottoman Empire.* The educational system in Turkey was created and monitored by the *Kemalism ideology*, which focused on teaching and hyping-up of Mustafa Kemal Ataturk - his beliefs, thoughts, and philosophy while glazing over other important events and characters in the rich history of Turkey and the land she occupies. In other words, Kemalism ideology was the idolization of Mustafa Kemal Ataturk, while quickly going over other subjects, such as the Ottoman Empire, and the other empires created and ruled by the Turkic peoples.

That was Turkey, let me write about Canada next and afterward, try to compare both countries.

In Canada, during my elementary, high school, and university years, I did not read or hear much about the country of Turkey or the empires ruled by the Turkic people.

I did not know that I missed out on anything, since, what is that universal phrase, *ignorance is bliss*, in other words, *what you do not know, will not hurt or affect you.* I went through the educational system in Canada, but I did not acquire any knowledge about my past, as there is another phrase, *if you do not know your past, you will not know your future.* This concerned me, the concern increased the more I realized, I did not know much about my past and about an empire that collapsed less than 100 years ago. This was an empire that my great grandparents were born into and I had seen personal identification documents that stated, *a citizen of the Ottoman Empire.* And I knew nothing about the empire, is that not interesting, bad, and sad, all at the same time.

Granted, in college and university, my focus was trying to finish a *Business of Administration* degree, therefore not seeing anything in my program regarding an empire that no longer existed was understandable. Furthermore, in elementary, it was not important enough to teach children about the empire, early in their education life, this was also understandable.

But, surely, in High School, I definitely should have been introduced to the Ottoman Empire. Additionally, I think back and realize that the following few questions could have been answered in high school since they are rather important, these were:
Was the empire not one of the participants in World War I, to be mentioned in Social Studies 10 course? I will answer this question by stating, yes the empire was one of the participants, sadly dragged into the war, for the benefit of the imperial powers.

Did the empire not influence Europe, Africa, and Asia, to be mentioned, in Psychology 20 course? I will answer this question as well, by stating that close to 40 nations came into existence, from the collapse of the empire, therefore, yes, the empire should have been mentioned and studied in detail.

Did *Ludwig Van Beethoven* copy the classical march theme titled, *Marcia Alla Turca*, from the empire, to be mentioned in the Music 30 course? The answer is yes, Beethoven was influenced by the Ottoman Janissary Marching Band, and wrote the classic march, and yes, the empire should have been cited in the studies.

The answers to the above questions and many more were found in many books read after graduating from university, sadly, they were not found while attending the educational system in Canada. Not trying to be too critical of the system, but trying to state the fact that the Canadian Education System, particularly, Social Studies and History courses were not diversified. The focus of my studies were on the United Kingdom, the Canadian and American civil wars, and the Commonwealth nations and unity.

Therefore, what I learned in Turkey, years and years prior in elementary and junior high school, were still very deep inside my mind, but I did not have any use to regurgitate the knowledge. The knowledge that was deep down there did not require reciting in my everyday life, since it was not useful while attending school, living, and working in Canada.

Years after finishing my university degree, I started reading about Turkey, since I had the time to read the topic which intrigued me, the favorite topic being - History. The more I read, the more I realized that there were areas that interested me the most, these were:
The collapse of the Ottoman Empire,
The creation of the Republic of Turkey,
Mustafa Kemal Ataturk,
The sultans of the empire and their relatives,
Colonialism,
Industrialism, and
Injustice actions by the imperial powers against the empire.

Also, the more I read and researched, the more I realized that the education I received in Turkey, years prior were coming to the surface, but, only in little bits and pieces.

Therefore, to the question, *who are you?* I'm Rid, and I strongly feel that I have knowledge and understand the subject, since I have years of focused reading, studying, and researching of the Ottoman Empire.

The subject of this story is my area of knowledge, that being the Ottoman Empire. However, the focus will be on the eldest son of a sultan, and the sultan himself. Both the eldest son and the sultan are explained briefly in the below paragraphs.

The sultan being, *Lawmaker Sultan Suleiman*, who ruled the empire during the empire's zenith years. He was untouchable, revered, and feared, but once looking past his mighty title, name, and qualifications, we realize that he made questionable decisions, one of them being the decision to order the execution of this eldest son.

And the eldest son being, *Prince Mustafa*, who was a prince with the most potential of any other prince, during the 600 plus year existence of the empire. Yes, I know that the last sentence is an extremely strong statement, but research does point to this fact - Mustafa was the prince with the most potential and the **hope** of the majority of the people living in and out of the empire to ascend to the throne.

Also, it would be beneficial for the western population, particularly, anyone living outside of Turkey to read the tragic and heartbreaking story of Mustafa from a person that knows the subject thoroughly, who will be without bias, and finally, who writes in the English language. The English language that he speaks fluently, and who is someone from this part of the western community.

Why are you writing this story?

There are lessons to be learned from the interactions of a sultan and his children, particularly, the sultan's interaction with his eldest son. Plus, it is still a relevant story even after 500 years have passed, and important lessons can be filtered out from this interaction between a father and his son.

Surely, this relationship between Sultan Suleiman and his eldest son Prince Mustafa is not learned in schools of the western world, whether, elementary, junior high, or high school. I should know, I went through the education system and the information written in this story is not thought.

Granted, if one were to attend a History Faculty at a university, surely, one would expect that parts of this story, will be thought in the program. But, I strongly suspect that the part about Prince Mustafa being executed by his biological sultan father, will not be in the literature, maybe a line or two, at the most will be in there.

Furthermore, the urge to write this story now is due to wanting to relay the information that is still an intriguing topic of conversation in other parts of the world, while in the western world, it is a topic that is seldom talked about, discussed, or studied.

Moreover, it will be beneficial to write a non-fiction story that will educate and entertain the esteemed readers, and introduce a high percentage of them, to a part of the world that they do not know much about. But, I have to clarify the above statement of, *a non-fiction story,* this story is not entirely non-fiction.

The story is a non-fiction telling of the Ottoman Empire, until the tale-end of Lawmaker Sultan Suleiman's time, in other words, chapters one to five, and chapter seven are true and well researched factual telling of the empire. Granted, it is a strong statement, which could be retorted by a reader, with one line that could show something other than what was written in this story. However, I am confident of the truth of the story, and I welcome any critique, therefore, bring on the criticism.

However, most everything in chapter six will be a fictional telling of what happened when Prince Mustafa rode into the Ottoman Empire's campsite, and entered the shadowy and eerie big black tent, where his sultan father was waiting for him in. Therefore, the readers will have an entertaining, interesting, and surprising chapter. But please, I urge you to not peek ahead.

There are books written that give detailed information of when Mustafa came to the front entrance of the black tent, but no factual information is available of what happened inside the tent. The reason for this is that no one knows what exactly happened in there.

Therefore, to the question of, *why are you writing this story?* The answer is that I feel compelled to tell this fascinating story to readers, who surely want a story about outrageous intrigue, manipulation from years prior, and refined culture from days long forgotten.

Will we learn anything more about Prince Mustafa, which we have not already known about previously?

The simple answer will be yes, there is always something to be learned from reading a book or story. In this story, I will explain the life of Prince Mustafa and the betrayal charges made against him by his sultan father.

Also, the part where Mustafa entered the black tent has been speculated by most everyone, but never fully known.

What I will do is take you back to October 6, 1553. What day was that? It was a Tuesday and bring forward previously unknown and intriguing events from that day, told in a fictional telling.

Therefore, the answer is - yes you will learn something new, which you have never been allowed or given the opportunity in your education system to learn before.

Enjoy,

CHAPTER ONE

Origins of the Turkic People

"Not all those who wander are lost." --- JRR Tolkien,

"His face, once as bright as the sun, is now set, his appearance and color ashen." --- Taslica Yahya (poem written for Mustafa)

"Time is a train, makes the future the past, leaves you standing in the station, your face pressed up against the glass." --- Lyrics from the song, Zoo Station, sung by the group named U2 (writers - Adam Clayton, Dave Evans, Larry Mullen, and Paul Hewson

Before beginning the story of *Prince Mustafa*, the protagonist, the **hope** of the people, the **hope** of the empire, and the son of *Sultan Suleiman*, it would be beneficial to start many centuries back, to the origins of the Turkic people. This early examination of the Turkic people will help the esteemed readers understand the culture and philosophy that made-up the core beliefs of the protagonist.

The central principles and values of the Turkic people evolved and developed throughout the centuries, to form the base of the protagonist's thought process during his lifetime. Furthermore, starting the story many centuries back will show how the Turkic people migrated from Central Asia and settled in Asia Minor, integrating and assimilating with others when necessary, and adopting principals and beliefs when required or obligatory. Therefore, this first chapter about the origins of the Turkic people is mandatory.

Like a bricklayer, who first builds a solid foundation, and after the foundation has set properly, unshakable, and indestructible, the bricklayer will add layers upon layers of heavy red brick to build up the solid and strong wall. Similarly, the author, who is known as a sentence-layer here (and attempts to be clever at times, without success) adds layers upon layers of sentences and paragraphs to build an enjoyable and satisfactory story. A good foundation will set a very good understanding of the proper and just light that needs to shine on the protagonist, and his Turkic origin. For this reason, as stated in the above paragraph, this first chapter is compulsory and mandatory, before we get into the juicy part, as the saying goes.

Now, the sentence-layer will begin with the first reference of the Turkic people in around the year 200 B.C.

The first historical reference to the Turkic people appeared in the Chinese records of around the year 200 B.C. Yes, you read that right, the first reference is not in Europe, Middle East, Anatolia, or Mesopotamia, it was from the most eastern country, the land of the rising sun. These records refer to a tribe called the *Tu-Kue* (Turkic) *Hsiung-Nu* (Hun), who were members of a nomadic Asian people. The Turkic Hun tribes lived in the area bounded by the following:
The lonely *Altai Mountain*,
Deep cold blue waters of *Lake Baikal*, and
The northern edge of the endless and hot *Gobi Desert*.

The references made in the Chinese records were due in part while building the *Great Wall of China* to protect the Chinese people from its enemies and invaders from northern Asia, where the nomadic tribes resided. These nomadic tribes were also comprised of Turkic Mongol groups that took part in the invasion of China.

Also, in the first references of these nomadic people, the terms *Turuk* or *Turkic* were used interchangeably to describe them. In this novel, especially in the first few chapters, the word Turkic will be used to describe these nomadic people.

To understand the origins of the Turkic people, we need to properly grasp and recognize the area of the world that the said people came from. The more we understand and learn about this area of the world - the difficult challenges faced, the strong partnerships formed, and the long journey tracked - the more we will know and appreciate the Turkic people and the story that is going to unfold and be told. Furthermore, it is best to give a very detailed explanation of the land, district, and territory mentioned, more precisely, the far-away lonely mountain, cold blue lake, and the endless hot desert.

The *Altai Mountain* is a mountain range in central and east Asia, where the countries of Russia, China, Mongolia, and Kazakhstan come together and are where the rivers named the *Irtysh* and *Ob* have their murky blue and green very cold waters collect. The name *Altai* in Mongolian means Gold, therefore, the mountain translates to English to mean the *Gold Mountain*.

In the Turkic languages, *Altin* also means Gold, which is believed to be another version of the reason of the *Altai* (*Altin*) (*Gold*) mountain name. However, it is still up for debate which nation gave this mountain range their name, the Mongolians or the pockets of Turkic people living in this area. Nonetheless, when the sun starts to set on the western horizon, and the sun-rays hit the Altai Mountain top at just the right angle, that is when the top of the lonely mountain shines as bright as the valuable and priceless gold jewel, hence the *Altai* name.

The northwest end of the Altai Mountain is where *Lake Baikal*, meaning the *Natures Lake* is located. *Lake Baikal* is one of the largest freshwater lakes by volume in the world, containing roughly fifteen percent of the world's unfrozen surface freshwater. Also, the lake is believed to be the world's deepest at 1,600 meters and oldest, estimated to be 25 million years old.

Lake Baikal was formed by constant rifts and movements on the surface of the earth that created a deep valley, hence, this was how the lake was formed. What is a rift lake, you ask? A rift lake is a lake that formed due to the result of the sinking of the ground due to the movements on fault lines. Therefore, Lake Baikal was formed by multiple movements and shakes from below the continental crust.

The Altai Mountain extends southeast, where it gradually becomes lower flatland that is fertile, and finally it merges into the distant high plateau of the *Gobi Desert*.

The Gobi, meaning *Semi Desert*, is a large region in Asia that covers northwest China, and southeast Mongolia. The Gobi Desert was notable in history as part of the great and glorious *Mongol Empire*, and as the passageway of several important cities along with the ever-important, and ancient network of trade routes that were for centuries central to cultural interaction along the far-reaching, and well-known *Silk Road*.

The fertile flatlands that stretched away from the Gobi Desert were the birth grounds of the Turkic people.

Specific references again in Chinese sources from the sixth century A.D., identifies that the tribal kingdom called Tu-Kue was settled near the *Orkhon River* southwest of the Gobi Desert, and south of Lake Baikal. In the reference, it states that the *Khan* (*chief*) of this tribe accepted the nominal dominance of the *Tang Dynasty* for protection during these times. This mighty Chinese Tang Dynasty was of an imperial scale that ruled China and her surroundings with ruthless and brutal conviction during these war-filled days. This is the period from the years 615 to 800 A.D., which is regarded as a high point in Chinese civilization, and the golden age of cosmopolitan culture in this far east country and territory.

Turkic people from this vast and eternal area around the Altai Mountain, Lake Baikal, and Gobi Desert region founded the *Gokturk Empire*, which was a confederation of tribes under a dynasty of khans whose influence extended during the sixth to ninth centuries. The Gokturk's, which means *Celestial Turks* were a community of several different nomadic peoples in this boundless area that would soon shape the culture, customs, and dominant beliefs of these scattered nomadic people.

The mighty *Byzantine Empire* enlisted the Gokturk's in the late seventh century as allies against the *Sasanian Empire* since the Turkic warriors were skilled at horse riding, bow and arrow shooting, and sword fighting. Interesting to note here, the Sasanians were recognized as one of the leading world powers and also was the last Iranian empire before the rise of the religion of Islam.

The Gokturk's protected the borders of the Byzantine Empire and this relationship between the said parties lasted for over two hundred years until the Turkic people began converting to the religion of Islam.

In the eighth century, another Turkic tribe, the *Oguz Turkmen* tribe formed the *Oguz State* in central Asia during this early medieval period. The name *Oguz* is a common Turkic word for *tribe*.

The Oguz State was located in western Asia from the territory of the Aral Sea, which lies between the countries of Kazakhstan and Uzbekistan, and to the land bridge known as *Transoxiana* (*Land beyond the Oxus river*).

The *Land beyond the Oxus river* was the portion from west to central Asia corresponding with the modern-day countries of Uzbekistan, Tajikistan, southern Kyrgyzstan, and southwest Kazakhstan land area; it is the region west of the *Oxus River*. The river flows from the northwest direction into the *Aral Sea*. In ancient times, the *Oxus River* was regarded as the boundary between Persia and the nomadic and obstinate eastern territory of the nomadic Turkic people.

This region was representative of the changing dynamics of the common people during these tumultuous times. The Turkic migrations after the eighth-century were part of a general movement of peoples out of Central Asia. The migration was influenced by several interrelated factors such as climatic change, the strain of growing populations on a fragile pastoral economy, and pressures from stronger and dangerous neighbors.

Among those caught up in this spirit of restlessness and anxiety on the fertile prairie lands were the *Oguz Turks*, who had embraced the religion of Islam in the tenth century and established themselves around the old city of *Bukhara* (current-day city in Uzbekistan). Humans have inhabited this ancient city of Bukhara for over five thousand years. Located on the ancient *Silk Road*, the city has long served as a center of trade, scholarship, culture, and religion in the Transoxiana region, under their leader named *Seljuk*.

Split by dissension, division, and disagreement among the tribes, one branch of the Oguz tribe went further east into western China, while the other, led by the descendants of *Seljuk*, went west, and entered service with the *Abbasid Caliphate* at the city of *Baghdad*.

What is a Caliphate? Caliphate means the supreme religious and political leader of the Islamic state. *Abbasid's* were the leaders of Islam during these times and were also the self-declared rulers of the age-old territories and countries of lower Mesopotamia, Syria, and, Persia. The *Abbasid Caliphate* succeeded to be the spiritual leader of the new religion of Islam, after the death of *Prophet Mohammed* (peace be upon him). The *Abbasid Dynasty* descended from Mohammed's youngest uncle, *Abbas Ibn Abd Al-Mutalib*, from whom the dynasty takes the name. The caliphs of this dynasty ruled this immense territory from their archaic, but the natural and refined capital city of Baghdad.

Known as *Gazi's* (*warriors of the Islamic faith or spiritual warriors*), the Turkic horsemen were organized in tribal bands to defend the entire frontiers of the caliphate, often against their very own troubled kinsmen, who were constantly in battle with one another for supremacy. In the year 1055 A.D., the *Seljuk Khan* named *Tugrul Bey* (*Bey* meaning *Sir*) occupied the capital city of Baghdad at the head of the mighty army composed solely of Turkic Spiritual Warriors and a smaller number of *Mam-luk's*, meaning - *slave-soldiers*, who were of Circassian, Armenian, Abkhazian, Georgian, and Kurdish. The indomitable and wilful Turkic, *Tugrul Bey* forced the caliphate to recognize him as the sultan (*king*) in Persia and all of Mesopotamia, and came to be known as the *Great Seljuk Sultanate*.

As the *Great Seljuk Sultanate* engaged in state-building, they eventually emerged as the champions of Sunni Islam against the Shia sect. Although Sunni Islam makes up the majority of Muslims, not every Muslim belongs to the same Islamic sect. A Muslim's Islamic beliefs may take one of the following forms, only the three largest sects within Islam are emphasized here now, however, there are many other smaller sects as well.

The Sunni sect of Islam, which means *Tradition*, makes up eighty to ninety percent of all Muslims in the world. Sunnis regard themselves as those who emphasize the traditions, lifestyles, and teachings of Prophet Mohammed and of the first three generations of the community of Muslims that followed the ways of the last prophet.

Shia sect of Islam, which means *Following*, comprises ten to fifteen percent of all Muslims. *Shiites*, as they are called, believe that Prophet Mohammed's son-in-law *Ali* was his designated successor. Ali was a highly important and influential individual that was believed to be designated as the next ruler of the Muslim community, by the last prophet. There is still a dispute in the Muslim community to this day whether Prophet Mohammed designated his son-in-law Ali as his successor (or not), however, this is another intriguing story for another project.

Upwards of five percent of the Muslims are *Sufis*, who are Islamic mystics. Sufis go beyond external requirements of the religion to seek a personal experience with God through forms of meditation and spiritual growth.

The champion Sunni sultan *Tugrul Bey's* successor was *Mehmet Ibn*

Daud, who was also known as *Alp Arslan* (meaning - *Lion Heart*). Alp Arslan was a big man of immense stature, both in myth and legacy, and in reality. The Turkic Spiritual Warriors who were free-spirited, but loosely under the rule and control of Alp Arslan, cut deeper and further into Byzantine Empire's massive territory in Anatolian lands to raid her prized possessions. The Spiritual Warriors would take booty from non-Muslims and returned the prizes to the rich Byzantine's in exchange for land for their own usage. This dealing between the free-fighting Spiritual Warriors and the Byzantine's eventually caused the opening up of the eastern frontier of Anatolia to the Great Seljuk Sultanate, who strode freely into the pristine and un-touched Asia-minor and took over the lands, without a fight - as the new landlords.

The statement, *without a fight* is not particularly accurate, as empires always fight one another, and eventually, the major clash between the Byzantine Empire and the Great Seljuk Sultanate would happen, this will be explained below.

Anatolia is a Greek word to mean *East* or *Sunrise* and it is located in the geography of *Asia-Minor*, which is another Greek word to mean *Small Asia*. Anatolia is the most western part of Asia, and it extends to the Bosporus narrow waterway, Marmara Sea, and Dardanelles Sea. More precisely, Anatolia sits on the land area and is bounded by the Black Sea to the north, the Mediterranean Sea to the south, and the Aegean Sea to the west.

Since the Great Seljuk Sultanate was driving further into Anatolia and advancing into the Byzantine Empire's territory, the two strong and dynamic empires were on a crash course for monumental bloodshed, for the eventual supremacy of the immaculate and natural Anatolian land.

Expectedly, the two massive and malevolent empires of the Seljuk's and the Byzantine's met in the summer of the year 1071 A.D. The Battle of Manzikert was fought at modern-day *Malazgirt* in the province of *Mus* in eastern Turkey. The decisive defeat of the

Byzantine army to the commanding officer - Alp Arslan and the capture of *Emperor Romanos IV Diogenes* played an important role in undermining Byzantine authority in eastern Anatolia and allowed for the gradual conquest of the entire Asia-minor by the Turkic people.

Emperor Romanos was a member of the Byzantine military aristocracy who, after marrying the widowed empress *Eudokia Makrembolitissa*, was crowned Byzantine emperor and reined from the years 1068 to 1071 A.D. (until the defeat at the Battle of Manzikert). During his reign, the main objectives of the emperor were to halt the decline of his military, increase income for the empire, and stop the Turkic incursions into Byzantine lands, however, these passionate wishes did not come to fruition.

The capture and return of Emperor Romanos by the Seljuk's to the Byzantine capital city of Constantinople started the end of his short, yet eventful regime. Emperor Romanos was kept captive in his palace at *Seraglio Point* of Constantinople and was eventually overthrown in a bloody coup and blinded to eliminate any possibility of him returning to power. The emperor died in the year 1072 A.D. and was buried at *Pantokrator Monastery*, which is located in the present-day neighborhood named *Zeyrek* (of Istanbul).

Within ten years of the bloody Battle of Manzikert, the Seljuk's won control of the precise jewel that was called Anatolia. Although successful in the west, the Seljuk Sultanate in the capital city of Baghdad reeled under attacks from the eastern Mongol tribes and was unable to continue to successfully exert authority directly with the eastern nomad peoples. Plus, the free-fighting Turkic Spiritual Warriors were carving small territories for their usage in Anatolia. The once-dominant and strong great empire in this region was starting to show weakness and vulnerability. The strongest of the Turkic Spiritual Warriors that emerged was the *Seljuk Sultanate of Rum*, a similar name, but a different empire altogether.

The meaning of the word *Rum* is interesting and deserves a lengthy and thorough explanation. In ancient times, the word Rum was used by the traveling Arabs to refer to the lands that were owned and ruled by *Rome (Rome* or *Roman) Empire*. In the Arab language, there is no o sound, and therefore any Latin pronunciation of the letter o was always spelled and pronounced with the letter u. Therefore, Rome came to be pronounced Rum, and the old Roman lands were described as Rum Lands. The pronunciation of Rum was carried over to the Turkic people and they too described the lands once belonging to Rome and Byzantine Empire as Rum Lands, in Turkish this was written as *Rumeli*. Therefore, the Seljuk Sultanate of Rum essentially meant the descendants of the old Seljuk Empire that ruled the timeworn old Roman lands.

This new Rum Sultanate with the capital at the ancient and timeless city of *Konya* gained the power to rule central Anatolia, while the weakened and vulnerable Great Seljuk Empire tried yet to dominate eastern Anatolia and beyond. During the eleventh century, Rum Sultanate attained a position of dominance over the other smaller and numerous Turkic states in and around Anatolia.

The success of the Sultanate of Rum in central to the west and the Great Seljuk Sultanate in eastern Anatolia stimulated a heavy-handed response from Europe in the form of the *First Crusade*. The bloody offensive of the First Crusade was launched in the year 1097 A.D. (only 26 years after the bloody Battle of Manzikert) by the Byzantine Empire with the aid of the European crusaders, which dealt the Sultanate of Rum a decisive and deathly defeat. The capital city of Konya fell to the European crusaders, who compelled the Rum's to provide them with reconnaissance, in the form of slaves. Since the Crusaders were going to march to the holy city of Jerusalem, and with the help from the slave Rum's, it was going to be beneficial for the eventual goal of capturing the divine city from the Arab Muslims.

In a matter of a few years with the help of the Crusaders and the campaigning that was mastered by the Byzantine Empire, this ageless empire restored its rule in the western portion of Anatolia.

A Turkic revival occurred in the early twelve century, and in the year 1140 A.D., the Rum's nullified many of the European Christian Crusaders' bloody gains (43 years after the First Crusade). During these tumultuous times, the greatest damage to Byzantine Empire's rule and territory loss was caused by their Christian brothers - the European Crusaders, who had commissioned another crusade, this being - the *Second Crusade*.

The Crusaders in the year 1204 A.D. attacked Byzantine Empire and occupied the capital city of Constantinople. The Crusaders sacked the capital city and declared this city as their new capital of the newly declared *Latin Empire*. A few independent territories of *Iznik*, *Trabzon*, and *Epirus* of the Byzantine Empire survived the on-slaughter from the newly created Latin Empire. The Turkic people allied with the Byzantine's in Anatolia against the Latin's, and in the year 1261 A.D., *Emperor Michael Palaeologus* of Iznik drove the Latin's from Constantinople and restored the rule of the Byzantine Empire.

The Sultanate of Rum survived to the late thirteenth century as a vassal and dependent of the Mongols, who had already subjugated the Great Seljuk Empire at Baghdad. The Mongols were the new powers in eastern Anatolia, however, this power and influence in the region only lasted until around the year 1330 A.D. From all this change of powers in a short time, this region around Anatolia saw much change with the smaller and multitude of Spiritual Warrior Emirates that competed for supremacy and dominance among each other.

From the chaotic conditions that prevailed throughout the Middle East, particularly in Anatolia, a new power emerged - that of the Ottoman Turks or the *Osmanli*.

Documentation of the early history of the Ottomans is scarce by western sources, however, available in a multitude in Ottoman Turkish if one can have them translated. According to some semi-legendary accounts, *Ertugrul*, who was a khan of the tribe called *Kayi*, of the Oguz Turks, had fled from Persia in the early thirteenth century to escape the Mongol hordes, and took service with the Sultanate of Rum in middle Anatolia. *Ertugrul Bey* (reigned from 1280 to 1299) was granted a small territory in western *Bithynia* facing the *Byzantine Empire's* borders around the city of *Bursa*.

The leadership of the tribe eventually passed to Ertugrul's son, *Osman* (reigned from 1299 to 1326), who was the eponymous founder of the Osmanli dynasty, which was better known in Europe as the Ottomans, and the empire was going to endure for over 600 years until the creation of the Turkish Republic in the year 1923.

Osman's small emirate attracted Spiritual Warriors who wanted to join in on conquests. The plunder from the conquests were divided equally, one half to the Spiritual Warriors, and the other half to Osman Bey. Osman, who eventually acquired the title of sultan, organized a politically centralized administration at the city of *Sogut*, which is in the *Bilicik* province of Turkey now. With the help of the Spiritual Warriors, Osman Bey facilitated a rapid territorial expansion around western Anatolia. The city of Bursa fell in the final year of his reign; in the year 1326, and become the capital of the newly formed empire. Osman's successor was his son named *Orhan* (reigned from 1326 to 1359), who crossed the *Dardanelles* narrow waterway in complete authority and established a permanent European base at *Gallipoli* in the year 1354.

Orhan's son was *Murad I* (reigned from 1359 to 1389) annexed most of the landmass known as *Thrace* (called *Tarakya* by the Turks) and encircled Byzantine's capital city of Constantinople from all sides. The capital city of the Ottomans moved now from

Bursa to *Adrianople* (present-day *Edirne*). In the year 1389, the Ottoman Spiritual Warriors defeated the Serbs at the *Battle of Kosovo*, where *Sultan Murad* lost his life. Nonetheless, the steady stream of Ottoman victories in the Balkans continued under Murad's son and now the current Sultan of *Yildirim* (meaning - *Thunderbolt*) *Beyazit I* (reigned from 1389 to 1403).

As the Ottoman's were preparing for the siege of Constantinople, they were confronted by the brutal Mongol hordes under the supreme rule of *Timur-Lenk* (Tamerlane), to whom many of the independent Spiritual Warriors defected since the Spiritual Warriors saw the might of the ruthless Mongolian ruler from the far east lands, and wanted to join this force. Mighty Tamerlane crushed the Ottoman forces near the current-day capital city of *Ankara* in the year 1402 and captured Sultan Beyazit I. According to legend, the sultan was displayed like a savage animal in a fancy designed iron cage. The unfortunate sultan lasted almost one year in captivity but eventually died in the year 1403. He left behind five adult heirs, who for over a decade competed amongst each other for complete control of what remained of the Ottoman Empire. The five heirs that fought each other until only one stood were: Mustafa, Mehmet, Isa, Musa, and Suleiman.

Recovery of Ottoman prestige was very slow, but Anatolia and the Balkans were gradually re-absorbed and re-conquered in the year 1420, with the sultan now being *Mehmet I* (reigned from 1413 to 1421).

Aside from scattered outposts in *Peloponnese* (current-day southern Greece land area), all that remained of the Byzantine Empire in the year 1420 was its (once) exquisite capital city of Constantinople - that was it. The city was cut off by land and sea; surrounded by the following:
Turks on the western lands, right beyond the magnificent protection of the high walls,
Marmara Sea on the south and east, and
Golden Horn body of water on the north, and the other side of the

narrow inlet of water, again were the Turks.

Despite long periods of truce with the Turks, it was evident and undeniable that a final battle would be taking place for the prestigious and precarious city. *Murad II* (reigned from 1421 to 1451) stepped down from the throne to retire to the southern Anatolian town of *Mersin* and allowed his son to become the ruler. On becoming sultan in the year of 1451, *Mehmed II* (reigned from 1451 to 1481) immediately planned the systematic reduction and elimination of Constantinople's formidable defenses, particularly the awe-inspiring walls that surrounded the magnificent city. The military campaign lasted for over one hundred days, nonetheless, ending on May 29, 1453, with the Turks fighting their way through the high walls and gates of the city, and ending the siege to a successful conclusion - Constantinople, the grand prize was now occupied by the Ottoman Turks.

News of the fall of Constantinople was heard with shock and horror in Europe.

Why was Europe shocked at the fall of Constantinople? For over a thousand years, this city was the gate-keeper of Europe, she alone stopped the flood of armies from the east, but unfortunately, she had fallen now, and the flood gates were open. The citizens of Europe were distressed and believed that the Turk's were soon to come to the outskirts of their faraway lands. But this did not happen, since the fall of Constantinople and the Byzantine Empire were an isolated military action, and did not have a complete critical effect on Europe - not for the time being.

Furthermore, to the Ottoman Empire, the capture of the imperial and regal capital was of supreme symbolic importance. Sultan Mehmed II, who was named *Fatih* (meaning - *Conqueror*) after successfully conquering Constantinople, was a man of culture and learning, as well as a superb warrior, who regarded himself as the successor of the Byzantine emperors, without a break in continuity. He made Constantinople, now known as *Istanbul*, from the

Greek phrase *Eis-Tin-Polin*, which literary means *to the city*, the capital of the Ottoman Empire as it had been for the Byzantine Empire, and he set about rebuilding her.

CHAPTER TWO

Sultan Suleiman's life and rule

"I am Suleiman the Magnificent. I AM the Ottoman Empire." --- Sultan Suleiman,

"He was open-hearted like the morning." --- Taslica Yahya (poem written for Mustafa)

"And let me try with pleasured hands, to take you in the sun to promised lands." --- Lyrics from the song, Time of the Seasons, sung by the group named Zombies (writer - R. Argent)

Sultan Suleiman was the absolute and dominant ruler of the Ottoman Empire from the years 1520 to 1566. He ruled the mighty empire until his death and was known as *Kanuni* (meaning - *Lawmaker / Lawgiver*) inside his massive and ever-expanding ruling territory. Furthermore, in the west, in the European continent, he was known and referred to as *Suleiman the Magnificent*. The Lawmaker, Magnificent Sultan Suleiman was the authoritative father of the son, Prince Mustafa; the prince had a rather unfortunate conclusion in a life that had immense and immeasurable potential.

The name Mustafa is originally Arabic, and it was the nickname of the prophet of Islam - *Prophet Mohammed*; Mustafa means the *Chosen One*. Similar to the prophet, the prince was also very much chosen as the future ruler of the Ottoman Empire.

Prince Mustafa was Suleiman's first son and based on this fact alone, he was the strongest candidate to eventually sit at the throne of an ever-expanding and mushrooming mighty empire.

The destined future ruler of the Ottomans was Mustafa. He was looked upon by everyone in and around *Topkapi Palace* (meaning - *palace of the sultanate*), plus the capital city of Istanbul as the eventual sultan. Therefore, Mustafa was brought up with the utmost care, passion, and love. Even though there were younger princes than Mustafa, and they were also well-loved by all, Prince Mustafa was still looked upon as the one, the future leader, and the future commander of the Ottomans.

The prince had much strength, plus support around him, to help him, and guide him to become the eventual ruling man, similar to his powerful father. However, sadly, there were forces at play that prevented his predetermined destiny.

Before preceding on the journey of learning about the prince, let us first learn about his father, and the Ottoman period under the father's rule, since this is a good start in this chapter where we will witness much happiness, but tragic and heart-breaking events were also present at the *Payitaht* (meaning - *home of the ruling family or dynasty*) or Topkapi Palace in Istanbul. Similarly, to chapter one, let us continue to lay the bricks on the foundation. Let us now continue the story where we left off; it is 41 years after the conquest of Istanbul.

Sultan Suleiman was born on February 6, 1494, in the city of Trabzon. This city is located on the Black Sea coast, precisely in the northeast area of Asia-minor. His mother was *Valide Hafsa Sultan*, (*Valide* - meaning *mother*) who was of Crimean origin and was born just outside the borders of the empire, in the city of Sevastopol.

Sultan Suleiman died inside his tenth on the battlefield, on a cold day of September 7, 1566, when he confronted, battled, and won the bloody war against the Hungarian Empire. It would be better stated that the Lawmaker died on his 13th military campaign one week before the victory was declared at the conflict titled, *Battle of Szigetvar*. Even though the battle was won, the ruler lost 20,000 *Janissary* soldiers from his 100,000 strong army, plus (more importantly to the Ottomans') the mighty empire lost valuable time, as the ultimate goal was to advance deep into Europe to capture the city of *Vienna*, back then referred to as the *Golden Apple*.

French diplomat and scholar named, *Cardinal Richelieu*, who studied years later of the bloody battle of *Szigetvar*, wrote the following about it in the year 1630, "The battle that saved civilization." The diplomat was referring to how the Ottomans' won the battle, but thankfully lost the strength and time to capture first and foremost the jewel of Europe, the city of Vienna, and afterward, the remainder of the continent.

Suleiman's father was *Yavuz* (meaning - *Stern*) Sultan Selim I, (reigned from 1512 to 1520) who also ruled the empire until his death, in the year 1520. Upon his father's death, Prince Suleiman road into Istanbul from his *sancak* (meaning - *seat of power or provincial governor*) located in the southwest Anatolian city of *Manisa*, where the mystic and sacred *Mount Sipylus* is located. He ascended to the Ottoman throne peacefully and without any struggle since he was the only surviving son of Stern Sultan Selim. Suleiman became the tenth sultan of the Ottoman Empire in the year 1520. Thus, with his reign, began the golden age of Ottoman history.

Suleiman's sultan father increased the Ottoman Empire's size by almost seventy percent during his short eight-year reign. Furthermore, Stern Sultan Selim, became the guardian of the pilgrimage routes to the important cities of Mecca and Medina, plus he was remembered as the first legitimate Ottoman sultan and Islamic Caliph.

Therefore, the new sultan had a difficult task of being compared to his sultan father, plus he had to try his best to outdo his father's good reputation. Italian historian *Paolo Giovio*, wrote the following about father and son, "The dauntless lion would leave his throne to a timid lamb." Venetian nobleman named *Monsieur Bar-*

tolomeo Contarini compared both sultans as "A courageous father of an even more courageous son."

Sultan Suleiman was described by Monsieur Bartolomeo Contarini, who witnessed the accession of the young ruler, and wrote the following regarding young Suleiman, "He is 26 years of age, tall, but wiry, and of a delicate complexion. His neck is a little too long, his face thin, and his nose aquiline. He has a shade of a mustache and a small beard; nevertheless, he has a pleasant appearance, though his skin tends to be a light pallor. He is said to be a wise lord, fond of study, and all men are optimistic for good from his rule."

Suleiman, who was intelligent, clever, and learned, plus a sound military tactician, expanded the Ottoman territory to include Christian kingdoms in eastern to central Europe and the south to east Mediterranean Sea regions. He started his conquests by first advancing onto the city of *Belgrade* in the year 1521, and afterward the Lawmaker embarked on a large-scale advance north of the *Danube River*.

Sultan Suleiman had many titles, here are some of the self-describing inscriptions, he used in official letters:
Slave of God,
Powerful with the power of God,
Deputy of God on earth,
The one who obeys the commands of the Quran,
Enforcer of the directions of the Quran,
Master of all lands,
The Shadow of God over all nations, and
Sultan of Sultans' in all of the lands.

It was very clear early on in his rule that Sultan Suleiman was not like his father, Stern Sultan Selim, who was a man of grim and strict nature. In describing the young ruler, his contemporaries noted his reasonable sense of understanding and equilibrium mindset in his character. Psychologically, his father's tough and forceful posture hurt the ruler, therefore he chose to have a calm and thoughtful approach to decision-making. Sultan Suleiman seldom, if ever showed impatience and anger in public.

Lawmaker Sultan Suleiman was at the forefront of the blossoming empire, with lands stretching deep into Europe, Asia, and northern Africa. When he reigned over the empire, both Muslims and Christians considered Suleiman the greatest leader of the world. The young ruler instituted major legislative changes within the empire that encompassed society, education, taxation, and criminal and civil law. He was also a brilliant military strategist, a devoted politician, and a great patron and protector of the arts. He was the sultan who ruled the Ottoman Empire at its height and left a huge and complex cultural and historical heritage not only to the Muslim civilization but also to the entire region.

The administrative institutions under the rule of Suleiman were taking shape and developing better alignments and ties than the reign of the prior sultans of the empire. At the top of the tiered Ottoman system was Sultan Suleiman, who acted as the overseer in political, military, judicial, social, and religious faculties. Officially, the sultan was called *padisah or sah*. Among Suleiman's Turk subjects, he was the nomadic warrior khan, a master of the tribal ruling class. For his Christian subjects, he was the Emperor. And for the Arabs under Ottoman rule, he was the imam (the religious leader), the protector of the religion of Islam. Only Suleiman appointed the official ruling high offices of the empire, and all legislation was issued by him in the form of a written decree with his *signature.*

Under the rule of Suleiman, the Ottoman expansion did not only encompass land, but also the sea as well, since the navy was given special priority. The sultan's navy, reinforced by corsairs, displaced the naval powers of Venice and Genoa in the eastern and central Mediterranean waters. Sultan Suleiman extended Ottoman rule southward by conquering lands in the Levant region of the eastern Mediterranean. The Levant regions are of the following countries (today): Cyprus, Egypt, Iraq, Israel, Jordan, Lebanon, Palestine, Syria, and southern Turkey.

Suleiman was called the Lawmaker by his subjects within the empire because of the new codification of law he implemented during his reign. Outside the borders of the empire, victory upon victory was the result against the Christian neighbors. Suleiman was a sensible statesman as well as a brave general. Ottoman forces confronted many different kings in Eastern Europe with great success in winning territories, plus signing alliance treaties with other nations that did not dare to provoke the empire. The following territories fell to Suleiman, during his reign:

The city and surroundings of Belgrade fell after a lengthy siege in the year 1521,

Many islands on the *Aegean Sea*, but most importantly, the island of *Rhodes* fell the following year,

In the year 1526, the Ottomans killed the king of Hungary *Louis II* at the *Battle of Mohacs* and took the capital of the Hungarian Empire named *Buda* (now known as Budapest),

In the summer of 1529, the city nicknamed *Golden Apple* (*Vienna*) was besieged, but did not fall,

By the year 1530, all of Northern Africa was brought under Ottoman rule, and

All of Mesopotamia was won from *Persia* in the year 1534.

All of the great cities of Islam were under the rule of the Ottoman Empire, these were: Mecca, Medina, Jerusalem, Damascus, Cairo, Urfa, and Baghdad.

The Ottoman Empire was an Islamic kingdom and most of the areas it had taken over previously from the Byzantine Empire had earlier been Christian. Therefore, for generation after generation, heirs to the Ottoman throne were the product of mixed parentage, born to wives or concubines of the sultan that came from many different ethnic groups that made up the massive empire, but ultimately the code of rule was of Islam in the lands of the empire (for most of the citizens).

From the very start, the Ottoman Empire had Turkish roots and rested on a grounded Islamic foundation, but it was an assorted mixture of ethnic groups and religious communities. Ethnicity was determined solely by religious affiliation. Muslims were thereby lumped together regardless of language or ethnic background and were the sultan's subjects. Because of the indivisibility of Islamic law and religious practice, it was inconceivable that Islamic law could be applied to non-Muslims. Under the system that was introduced during Sultan Suleiman's rule, non-Muslim groups were recognized as *millets* (different religious communities) and granted a degree of autonomy in their communal affairs and allowed to operate schools, religious establishments, and courts based on their customary law.

The structure of the empire during Suleiman's rule was formulated distinctively as following: The inner-circle composed of the sultan, his family, his harem, and his attendants. The outer-circle included high-ranking government officials, military commanders, landholders, bureaucrats, and Islamic scholars. Collectively, all members were known as soldiers, this system reflected the influence from the tribal mythology brought from middle Asia.

Lawmaker also held the title of caliph, which meant that Suleiman was the leader of the Islamic world. The important claim came from his overwhelming power, plus his status as guardian of the Holy cities of Mecca, Medina, Jerusalem, Baghdad, and Constantinople, therefore, a rightly claim indeed.

The Lawmaker wrote exquisite poems that were considered among masterpieces by many intellects. Artists, philosophers, academics, and religious leaders found refuge at his court. Suleiman was highly intellectual and fluent in many languages; these were as following: Ottoman Turkish, Arabic, Crimean, Persian, Italian, Latin, and Serbian.

Suleiman's laws set the character and policy of the empire for over three centuries after his death. He was the first and foremost reason the Ottomans enjoyed what was later on to be referred to as the *Golden Age* of the empire. From the start of the 1500s, the Ottoman Empire flourished and prospered in architecture, fine arts, gold mining production, and literary wisdom.

The term Lawmaker has precise importance in the context of the empire, and the Muslim traditions of the time. The laws that were set forth and derived from the *Quran* were applied universally in all the lands. Plus, Suleiman launched laws ancillary and supportive to the holy book that was tailor-made to the lifestyles of the changing dynamics of the empire.

Sultan Suleiman was no ordinary leader, witnessed by writer and diplomat for the Habsburg and Austrian Monarch *Monsieur Ogier Ghiselin de Busbecq*. The diplomat also served as ambassador to the Ottoman Empire, wrote the following precise warning of Europe's imminent conquest, "Onside are the resources of a mighty empire, strength unimpaired, habituation to victory, the endurance of toil, unity, discipline, frugality, and watchfulness...Can we doubt what the result will be...when the Turks have settled their conflict with Persia, they will fly at our throats, supported by the might of the whole East, how unprepared we are, I dare not say."

After expanding the empire and accomplishing ambitious ventures, the Lawmaker favored less warlike foreign policy. In connection with this policy, the Ottoman plan shifted from expansion to regional objectives. Sultan Suleiman was tired of waging war on the neighbors on all sides of the empire, he preferred to stay at the palace of the ruling family in Istanbul for almost all of the year and spent a few months in the winter at *Adrianople*, where he rested in isolation, away from numerous monitoring eyes.

Moreover, the Lawmaker's sons were growing and he was witnessing the increasing tension between the male heirs and their mothers, which concerned and feared him. Therefore, due to the tensions, Suleiman did not wish to leave Istanbul for long periods, as he believed that his throne would be in jeopardy, and surely he would be deposed.

The Lawmaker continually resided in Istanbul and lived a life away from the public eye. Moreover, he left the administration of the empire to his grand vizier, this concerned the janissary army, as a large percentage of the army preferred a visible sultan that wanted to secure the borders.

The Venetian ambassador Bernardo Navagero corroborates this fact and stated the following, "Because of age and the many accomplishments that made him a worthy successor under his past - having seized Rhodes and Belgrade, having driven the unlucky king of Hungary from his rule and life, and having won many regions in the Persian borders - Suleiman chose, not without good reason, to maintain peace. It is clear that in this last war in Transylvania with the most serene king of the Romans (Ferdinand of Austria), the sultan several times admitted with regret that things had gone too far. In sum, it is reasonably believed, as I say, that the sultan from now on will abhor war and will not resort to it unless he is forced, and then neither by his hand nor by his person, but by the hand of others - just as this year."

Sultan Suleiman had many concubines, and of the many, two of the females were the most important ones since they provided the ruler with male heirs to his throne. The first woman to bear a male child was *Mahidevran* (meaning - *one who is always beautiful*) *Gulbahar* (meaning - *rose spring*) Sultan, who gave birth to Prince Mustafa, the eldest child of Suleiman. Mahidevran was of Albanian origin, and she came from a wealthy family that gave consent for her to become the wife of the ruler. The birth of Mustafa was particularly important because he was born in the year 1515, which was 5 years before Prince Suleiman ascended to the Ottoman throne.

The second female who bore male heirs for Sultan Suleiman was named *Hurrem* (meaning - *one who is cheerful*) *Haseki* (meaning - *chief wife*) Sultan. This young beautiful woman was a captured slave girl from the south-east section of Poland, where the country borders Ukraine. Hurrem Sultan's real name was believed to be *Aleksandra Ruslana Lisowska*, and the following were the sons of Hurrem, they were: Mehmet, Beyazit, Selim, and Cihangir. The important matter here was that all of his children from Hurrem were born while Suleiman was the sultan of the empire.

Were there other children of Suleiman, by other concubines? Yes, there were, however, other children did not live past puberty, therefore, the focus is on the listed children from Mahidevran and Hurrem.

The Lawmaker loved Hurrem, the mother of all of his sons (other than Mustafa), and a poem was written by him, by his pen-name *Muhibbi* (meaning - *Amicable lover*) proves his devotion for her with the following verses:
"Throne of my lonely niche, my wealth, my love, my moonlight.
My most sincere friend, my confidant, my very existence, my sultan; the most beautiful among the beautiful.
My springtime, my merry-faced love, my daytime, my sweetheart, laughing leaf.

My plants, my sweet, my rose, the only one who does not distress me in this world.
My Istanbul, my heart, the earth of my Anatolia. My woman of the beautiful hair, my love of the slanted brow, my love of eyes full of mischief. I'll sing your praises always. I, lover of the tormented heart, Muhibbi of the eyes full of tears, I am happy."

In the Ottoman tradition, starting in the year 1451, during Sultan Suleiman's great-grandfather, *Conqueror* Sultan Mehmet II's rule, there was a law put into place called *Fratricide of a Prince*. This law stated that, "It was *appropriate* to strangle and kill all the male siblings of the newly crowned sultan, whatever their age was. Every one of the prince's siblings can be killed, until only the chosen prince remained, to become the new sultan."

The law of governance by the sultan imparted the right of executing the male members of his family to prevent an interregnum. What is an interregnum? This is when a few individuals fight against each other to become the sole ruler of the empire. The fratricide was a method to prevent a possible revolt or even war between surviving sons of the sultan.

Before this law, and before Sultan Mehmet II's rule, there were always bloody and costly battles on the field between the surviving princes, where this war would cause break-up and splitting-up of the empire.

A good example of when the empire broke apart due to having too many sons ready to assume the throne was *The Battle of Ankara*. The Battle of Ankara in the year 1402 decimated the empire, particularly the lands in Anatolia. During this battle, Thunderbolt Sultan Beyazit, died in captivity at the hands of the warlord Tamerlane of the Timurid Dynasty.

The Battle caused major division within the Ottomans as the territories of the crushed empire were divided among the surviving sons of Thunderbolt Sultan Beyazit.

Thunderbolt had five sons, these were, Mustafa, Mehmet, Isa, Musa, and Suleiman. Each son divided the empire into equal pieces to rule it. The five sons battled each other constantly for years to gain sole possession and power of the empire. The customary contest of trying to kill each other and gain their lands continued for many troubled years. These were tumultuous times for the sons of the Ottomans.

In the year 1412, *Celebi* (meaning - *Gentleman*) Sultan Mehmet I, rallied almost all of the surviving Ottoman chiefs and killed his brothers to allow him to have a firm grip on the throne of the empire. The lands of the empire were reunited once again, however not at the same size and might as previously.

The unfortunate battles between the sons of Thunderbolt Sultan Beyazit was referred to and discussed in length when the decision during Conqueror Sultan Mehmet II's rule (Grandson of Mehmet I). The decision was made that *all sons of the sultan, except the one with the most potential, can be murdered for the sake of the longevity and survival of the empire.*

When we sit today and look at this past practice, some may conclude that fratricide was brutal, unnecessary, and horrific. Those who argue for or against fratricide are right in their decision when debated properly and in full. Nonetheless, this act of killing a child was a crazy and sobering decision made for the survival and longevity of the empire, at the sacrifice of many many innocent and sinless princes.

The longevity of the empire was the utmost important matter, therefore sons could be sacrificed indeed, and ultimately sons had been sacrificed over each succession of a new ruler.

The sons of Suleiman who were ready to assume the throne when and if called upon were as follows (listed in order of birth): Mustafa, Mehmet, Selim, Beyazit, and Cihangir.

These mature men and siblings were heading into a maze of unknown intrigue and cunning; one of the princes would be called upon to be the ruler, at the expense of the others.

The oldest of Sultan Suleiman's children was Prince Mustafa; therefore, he was the closest and most reasonable choice as the son to assume the throne. The choice of Mustafa becoming the ruler was also recognized due to his wisdom, talent, and friends he kept, friends who were near his father the sultan. However, history did not play out this way. History took a turn that was unexpected, un-imagined, and un-thinkable by not only the mother of the prince but by the millions of citizens living inside the Ottoman Empire.

When the realization set into everyone inside the web of Suleiman's family that the next ruler would need to kill ALL of his siblings, the lead-up to the exchange of the ruler (the throne) became more worrisome, troublesome, and even elusive.

This story you are reading is well researched by the sentence-layer. He is a person who is well read in the subject matter of Ottomans, from both Turkish and Western perspectives.

He will bring forward his research and findings of the ascension of the ruler, after Lawmaker Sultan Suleiman, the Magnificent. The respected readers will need to understand that these were tumultuous and cunning times where if one prince become the sultan, the others (his brothers) would need to meet their death, and be murdered. Also, the readers will need to fully understand that all the sons were ready to become the next ruler of the empire. The simple fact was, shroud partnerships, wicked villainous gestures, and back-room secret handshakes among the elite were made. The elite, who had a lot to lose and much to gain by aligning with one prince, sponsored and supported him, over the others.

This non-fiction story you have in your hand is not without plenty of intrigues, suspense, and heartache. The focus of the story is the life of Prince Mustafa, with his immediate family and friends.

CHAPTER THREE

Mother to a Prince

"Shall I compare thee to a summer's day?" --- *William Shakespeare,*

"The sun of his beauty set, his council dissolved." --- *Taslica Yahya (poem written for Mustafa)*

"Midnight brought us sweet romance, I know all my whole life through." --- *Lyrics from the song, Midnight, the Stars and You, sung by Ray Noble and his Orchestra and Al Bowlly (writers - Harry M. Woods, Jimmy Campbell, and Reg Connelly)*

Let us now write about the life and times of the mother of Mustafa, who was named Mahidevran; and continue in the skillful trade of adding layers of sentences and paragraphs to solidify the story before an intense examination of the protagonist, the **hope** of the people, the **hope** of the empire, and the oldest son of *Sultan Suleiman.*

Mahidevran Gulbahar Sultan was born in the year 1500; this date was in question for some time, but as of writing this story, the date has come to be accepted as the accurate birth date for her.

Like almost every woman who entered the harem in Topkapi Palace in Istanbul, there is very little to no precise information about Mahidevran's early life. She found herself in the small-sized city of *Manisa* as one of the women in Prince Suleiman's courtship. Mahidevran eventually became Suleiman's favorite companion by the time she was 15 years old. Her real name was either *Malhurub Baharay* or *Rosne Pravane*, however, when she entered the harem in Manisa, the name Mahidevran was given to her by none other than Suleiman, as she was a strikingly beautiful young lady.

The sentence-layer would like to elaborate fictitiously about Mahidevran's striking beauty by writing the following, as this is how the readers should envision her. To put it with perfect simplicity, Mahidevran was a beautiful young lady, with beautiful facial and bodily features that were pleasing to the onlookers.

One could say she was a stunning young lady, the kind in any high school, when the prettiest student walked the hallway, going from one class to the next, all the able boys would turn to get a glimpse of the magnificent creature. That is how the readers should try to picture her. If this is difficult for some readers, as in they want a description of Mahidevran, instead of trying to come up with the high school analogy, then we will try to satisfy them, by explaining further about her.

In many works, readers surely have noticed that writers always invent a flaw in a character, maybe because they think real beauty is a stereotype, or because they think a flaw makes the character more realistic. So she will be beautiful except her upper lip is too thin, or her nose is a little too flat, or maybe she is flat-chested. There is always something.

Mahidevran was beautiful, with no true qualifications. Her skin was light beige to glowing light brown and impeccable; a perfect natural color. She stood about 170 centimeters, tall for a lady during these times, and her figure was firm, with high breasts, a small waist that looked as if one could almost put two hands around it, nice hips, good long legs. Beautiful face, erotic, smooth figure, artistically flawless, without a thin upper lip, or a flat nose, or a wrong bump, or bulge anywhere. To her admirers, particularly Suleiman during the years at the city of Manisa, she was not dull at all; she was perfect.

Was she that pretty? Yes, she was very pretty, more so than the sentence-layer is capable and able to describe.

Her ethnic background is a matter of controversy still. She was originally from either of the territories of Albania or Circassia, however, the more accepted narration was that she was from the Balkans region, just outside the borders of the Ottoman Empire.

Mahidevran's father was named *Abdullah Abdurrahman*, who was believed to be Christian by birth and converted to the religion of Islam. Abdullah was a boy that was brought into the janissary system as a child and rose steadily among the janissary ranks.

Not much is known about Mahidevran's mother, other than her name was either *Nazan Begum* or *Hatun Giray*, and she lived in the years, 1470 to 1520.

Mahidevran was the chief companion of Suleiman for a few solid years and the mother of Prince Mustafa; she gave birth to him in the year 1515 at the city of Manisa. She was listed among the seventeen women of the harem of Prince Suleiman, while he was the governor of Manisa, which is located in southwest Turkey.

In 1520, after the death of Suleiman's father, Stern Sultan Selim, the son moved to Istanbul to succeed his father as the new heir of the Ottoman Empire; his considerable court from Manisa followed with him. Mahidevran continued to be the chief consort and companion of Suleiman at the capital city of Istanbul since she was the mother of the only prince of the empire.

An important matter to state is that she gave birth to Mustafa at the age of 15, while Suleiman was just a prince and the governor of Manisa. The regular practice of the Ottomans was to send the princes away to distant lands to govern that city and territory and learn and mature into being a natural leader. Conversely, if and when the time came for the prince to be heir to the throne, he would be ready to be the sultan and rule the empire accordingly.

Foreign observers of the Ottoman family, especially the ambassadors of the *Venetian Republic* followed the sultanates dynamics closely. The comments made by the observers were extremely gracious and positive about Mahidevran's vital role as the prince's mother and of her devotion to his welfare that held a religious zeal. *Pietro Bragadin*, who was the ambassador in the early years of Suleiman's reign, reported that while both were still residents in the Topkapi Palace in Istanbul, Mustafa was her mother's "Whole joy."

However, more or less, anything further about Mahidevran has more myth and legend than an accurate telling of her life, since the truth of the matter was that little is known of her, and we get to know her by her interactions with her only son Mustafa, plus the rivalry she had with Hurrem Sultan.

Sultan Suleiman's harem was strictly secluded and guarded by male eunuchs, plus ruled by strict hierarchy enforced by the *High ranking female attendants in the harem*, to protect and guard the beautiful young ladies that were placed there to serve only the sultan, and his secret pleasures.

A newly acquired slave girl for Suleiman was first taken to the close proximate *Hamam* (meaning - *bathhouse*) of the Topkapi Palace, where she was inspected in full for an obvious illness or ailment. Afterward, if the young maiden was healthy, she was cleaned thoroughly, oiled, massaged, groomed, and lastly clothed. Finally, the cumbersome training began under the supervision of the high-ranking female attendant; the training included many subject matters such as: speaking Ottoman Turkish, dancing, singing, playing a musical instrument, reading literature and philosophy, erotic behavior techniques, and finally the religion of Islam. After the maiden had become the master of the subject matters, the sultan's mother, Valide Hafsa Sultan would carefully pick the best young woman for her sultan son, in this case, Sultan Suleiman.

Unlike in Europe, where the royal families married into other royal families from different kingdoms to make strategic alliances, in the Ottoman Empire, the sultans used slave girls for procreation and companionship. This practice was used to ensure that there would not be any distant family outside of the royal family to gain prominence or aspire for power in the empire. Moreover, the established imperial harem principle of *one concubine mother equals one son* was designed to prevent both the mother's undue influence over the sultan and the feuds with the blood brothers for the throne. The readers will soon understand that most of the set, age-old rules put in place in the harem, did not apply to the slave girl named Hurrem.

Furthermore, as can be expected, there was intense rivalry between the maidens of the harem to lure the sultan for an invite - an invite from the sultan into his bed. The slave girl who was lucky enough to bear the sultan a son was clothed in silks, brocades, and furs, and received the title of *Headmistress*. Therefore, the slave girl with the sultan's son was no more a slave; she would have a title, and live very comfortably afterward in her quarters, and receive a hefty salary. What is more, if the son become the next sultan, she would be the mother of the sultan, with unequaled power, control, and wealth in the empire.

Let us think about this for a minute. A harem is a place; right next door to the sultan's thrown, with multiple women, who are in constant competition among each other, trying to impress the mother of the sultan to secure a night with the sultan. The intrigue, plotting, secrecy, and trickery were non-stop until a male heir was provided. But, even when the heir had arrived, the plotting, surely never stopped, as it only got further complex and complicated in the days and years living in and around the harem, as the readers can see, the word harem, spelled backwards is *Madhouse*.

Mahidevran's stature as the chief companion of Sultan Suleiman was without argument true since she was the mother of Prince Mustafa, the eldest surviving son of the reigning sultan and the most potential heir to the throne. Also, she was second in importance after Valide Hafsa Sultan, the mother of Suleiman and the person in charge of the family affairs within the sultanate. This very important position, as second in command in the family, changed drastically once a certain slave girl named Hurrem, entered the harem in Istanbul and caught the eye of Suleiman.

Hurrem became one of the most powerful and influential women in Ottoman history and a famous, but controversial figure during the era she lived in. She achieved great power and influenced the politics of the empire through her husband, and played an active role in the affairs at the Topkapi Palace.

Why did Suleiman change much harem practices of the sultanate for his love for Hurrem? The answer was that these two persons were ideally matched to each other in character and temperament. Hurrem's main asset was her mind, plus she was able to entertain Suleiman with clever and witty talk and give good and sound advice on current affairs. Due to her intelligence, she became Suleiman's chief adviser on matters of the state and had a considerable influence upon internal affairs and international politics.

Hurrem Sultan gave birth to her first son named Mehmet in the year 1521, which officially displaced Mahidevran as the *mother of the only son*, and began the decline of Mahidevran's role in the sultanate. Furthermore, much to everyone's surprise, Hurrem got pregnant a few more times, and gave birth to a daughter named *Mihrimah* in 1522, and then a second son named *Selim* in 1524.

The rivalry between the two mothers who had given birth to princes never ended fully; it just escalated as the years passed.

Soon after, Hurrem became the new chief companion of Suleiman, and therefore Mahidevran's position within the family deteriorated further to be the ex-companion of Sultan Suleiman, which was not good news for her, as Suleiman stopped engaging in companionship with her. However, it could not be argued that she, Mahidevran, retained the status of the mother of Suleiman's eldest son, therefore her importance within the sultanate remained yet. Furthermore, Mustafa was an immensely popular prince while living in Istanbul. When he was only nine years old, the Venetian ambassador and traveler named *Luigi Bassano* reported that, "he has extraordinary talent, he will be a warrior; is much loved by the janissaries, and performs great feats."

It should be noted that Hurrem went on to give birth to two more sons, these were: Beyazit in 1525 and Cihangir in 1531.

This meant that Prince Mustafa, the only son of Mahidevran, had four princes to eventually compete with, for the Ottoman throne; all of the other princes were the sons of Hurrem.

Traditionally, the rule of *one concubine mother equals one son* was followed, what does this mean? This means the *One Son Rule*. The tradition followed in the empire was that when a concubine in the harem gave birth to a male heir, she would be removed from the harem, and given her own residence. She would be given a title and her sexual contact with the sultan would almost stop altogether. She would be forced to only focus on her son, groom him, and raise him to become the next sultan.

If the concubine gave birth to a daughter, her sexual relations with the sultan would continue until she gave birth to a boy.

But, as stated a few paragraphs back, the centuries-old laws and rules of the imperial harem did not apply to Hurrem, since she gave birth to multiple male heirs, which was never seen before. Plus, she did not take up residence outside of the Topkapi Palace. Hurrem stayed very close to the sultan, almost in the same wing as the palace.

Hurrem was a highly intelligent young maiden that understood the intrigue and plotting required to survive and thrive in the harem, against all other concubines. She grasped the horrific fratricide practice immediately, that being, if any other prince (Mustafa), other than her boys became sultan, it would be the death of them. Therefore, Hurrem maneuvered to stay close to Sultan Suleiman to keep herself and her children safe.

Hurrem was widely believed to be a wicked witch at Topkapi Palace, who had put a hypnotic spell on Suleiman. At the time, this witch theory was not farfetched and elaborated on outside of the palace.

There was the following account, told to writer and diplomat for the Habsburg monarch, *Monsieur Ogier Ghiselin de Busbecq*, in the year 1554, by religious elderly women of the capital city. The elderly religious women supplied Hurrem with bones to cook from the skulls of horses, donkeys, and wild boar, which were believed to be a very strong aphrodisiac when given to the victim; the victim being Suleiman.

After investigating the claims told to him by the elderly religious women, *Busbecq* wrote the following, "but none of them (elderly woman) agreed to sell these bones to me saying they were meant exclusively for Hurrem Sultan who, they said, made Sultan Suleiman continuously attached to her by making love potions and other magic means."

It was disgracefully witnessed that Suleiman was very obedient to Hurrem, he was similar to a six-year-old boy attached to his mother's skirt, surely, many believed that the magic spell that she put on him was working perfectly fine.

Hurrem aligned with different powers to eliminate those in power; those who did not see the future in parallel with her. One example of this elimination was the high-ranking individual of - the *Grand Vizier Pargali* (meaning - *from the town of Parga* in Greece today) *Ibrahim Pasha*, who openly supported Prince Mustafa's rise to the throne. Pargali Ibrahim was executed in the year 1536, for supposedly trying to replace Sultan Suleiman as the next sultan of the Ottoman Empire. This false accusation was labeled onto Ibrahim by those in close relationship with Hurrem, due to the Ibrahim's open support for Mustafa to the throne.

The execution of Ibrahim Pasha will be described in detail at a later period in this story.

As we know now, the Ottoman tradition was to expect all of the princes to train as provincial governors, which was part of their preparation for the throne. Besides, the prince's could only return to the Topkapi Palace, at the ascension to the throne, after the death of the current sultan, their father.

There was no formal designation to the throne. Once the new sultan's ceremony of *handing the sword* had taken place, his brothers were searched, found, and strangled. This cold system of fratricide ensured the longevity and stability of the Ottoman realm.

Mustafa, at the age of 17, was sent to Manisa in 1533, accompanied only by his mother. There were two reasons why the prince was sent for governor's duty. The first reason was obvious, in that, his age permitted for the training to govern a district to begin. The second reason was as follows, one spring day, Hurrem and Mahidevran got into another nasty screaming and hair-pulling fight, where the latter written maiden won on that particular day. To punish Mahidevran, the victor, Suleiman banished her to Manisa with their son Mustafa. Officially, it was not called an exile; rather it was portrayed as the traditional beginning for the training of the heir apparent.

The readers will remember that Sultan Suleiman also governed this city when he was a prince. Furthermore, this city was the birth location of Mustafa; therefore, the significance is rather uncanny as this location was a stopover for an eventual sultan in the making. Additionally, Manisa was the most important city and province for a prince to govern because according to tradition, only the favorite prince was appointed to this area. In conclusion, it was not as bad an outcome for Mahidevran and her son, as it could surely have turned out.

As soon as Mahidevran left Istanbul with Mustafa for Manisa, Hurrem and Suleiman got married in a grand ceremony. The marriage officially reduced Mahidevran's role to be an outsider within the family dynamics now. However, Mahidevran was the mother of the sultan's firstborn son, and therefore, Mahidevran still believed she held important significance and standing in the sultanate family.

Mahidevran was at the head of Mustafa's princely harem in Manisa, she endeavored to protect Mustafa from political rivals, as the ultimate goal was to guide him to become the next sultan of the empire. She most certainly maintained a network of informants in the capital city to provide her with information to keep her up-to-date in the current affairs at the Topkapi Palace.

Describing Mustafa's governor court, the Venetian ambassador of *Luigi Bassano* wrote that the prince had, "a most wonderful and glorious court, no less than that of his father," and the ambassador went on further to state, "his mother, who was with him, instructs him in how to make himself loved by the people."

During their time in Manisa, Mahidevran was known for her constant protection of her son, and she dedicated her own life to take care of Mustafa. She warned him constantly that he should make sure to maintain his governorship so that his citizens should never be unhappy with him. Eventually, the citizens of Manisa and the surrounding area cherished Mustafa, plus the remainder of the Ottoman people heard of his just rule and envisioned him to be the next ruler of the empire.

Another ambassador named *Bernado Navagero*, described Mahidevran's efforts to protect her son as follows, "Mustafa has with him his mother, who exercises great diligence to guard him against poisoning and reminds him every day that he has nothing else but this to avoid, and it is said that he has boundless respect and reverence for her," and he went on further to state, "it is impossible to describe how much he is loved and desired by all as the successor to the Ottoman throne."

Furthermore, Mustafa was receiving foreign ambassadors as well as high ranking Ottoman commanders regularly in his governorship, without his sultan father's knowledge. Plus, the visitors regarded Mustafa as an important ally against the Ottoman ruler. Habsburg Empire's ambassador Monsieur Ogier Ghiselin de Busbecq, who had visited Mustafa first, before entering Suleiman's court at Topkapi Palace, informed his emperor on his return to his country, "Mustafa will be an excellent sultan, receptive and open to talks." Suleiman, upon hearing of the ambassador's visit to Mustafa first was not amused, additionally, this action by the ambassador strained the relationship between the two mighty empires for a considerable time.

Hurrem, who was hearing that Mustafa was much loved by all, particularly the janissaries, constantly conspired against him to cause unrest by spreading propaganda and false statements. She caused the unrest to protect her sons and help one of them to the throne. Another obvious concern by Hurrem was that if Mustafa became the next sultan, then she and her children would swiftly be disposed of as this was the common practice of killing all the male siblings of the newly crowned sultan, whatever their age was, every one of the prince's siblings were killed. Therefore, as a mother, Hurrem, rightly so, had to use any means she felt necessary to keep Mustafa from becoming the next sultan.

Hurrem learned the art of becoming a master manipulator and used techniques such as emotional falsification, collusion with others, and bribery to bend many persons to her will. She learned how to play the game, and played it very well. In the end, Mahidevran suffered considerably from the games played by her rival; an example of this is explained below.

In 1541, when Prince Mehmet (Hurrem's firstborn son) reached the age of 16, he was ready to be a governor. What happened next was unexpected for Mahidevran and Mustafa. The eldest son, Mustafa, was transferred to the governorship of the city of *Amasya* from Manisa. Mehmet took over the governorship of Manisa, as it was written previously, Manisa was the most important city and province for a prince to govern, because according to tradition, only the favorite prince was appointed to this area; it was the stepping-stone to the throne.

Hurrem had used her considerable influence and power on Suleiman to remove the sultan's firstborn son from the governorship of Manisa to a lesser-known location of Amasya.

Amasya was one of the farthest provinces from the capital city. This move from Suleiman (most believe this move was forced onto Suleiman by Hurrem) was a clear sign to show that Mustafa might be the oldest son, but he was not the favorite one for the throne - in the eyes of his sultan father.

It should be stated that Hurrem, unlike Mahidevran never left the capital to accompany her sons for their governorship training. Hurrem always stayed next to Sultan Suleiman. This was an unmatched advantage Hurrem held over her rival Mahidevran, and another law and rule of the imperial harem that did not apply to Hurrem, but enforced and applied to Mustafa's mother.

When Suleiman left the capital city for military campaigns against the neighbors of the empire, Hurrem was left in charge to oversee the palace matters, head state affairs, deal with foreign emissaries, and even be his eyes and ears gathering information for him. She explained to Suleiman of the latest news through her constant stream of letters, which interspersed with romantic poems.

One such letter reads as follows, "My lord, your absence has kindled a fire in me that cannot be put out. Take pity on my suffering soul and write a letter to me as soon as you can so that I could find at least some consolation in it. My lord, I pray that when you read these words, your wish to write to us will be fortified and you will express all your longing to see us again. When I read your letter, your son Mehmet and your daughter Mihrimah were close by my side and tears were rolling down their eyes."

Suleiman's response was as follows, "at last we shall unite in souls, in thoughts, in imagination, in will, in heart, in everything that I have left of mine in you, and have taken of you with me, o my only love!"

The move of displacing Mustafa from Manisa to Amasya, did not reduce the love the people had for the eldest son. Mustafa, despite everything, was still the favorite of the army (janissaries), governors, most (if not all) of the grand viziers, and the citizens of the empire.

The fact was clear that Sultan Suleiman was afraid of Mustafa's escalating power within the empire; plus, the sultan was not ready to step down from the throne, he would remain there for years to come until the year 1566. That was a total of 46 long and tumultuous years. Lawmaker knew that Mustafa was much loved by all, plus a talented soldier, intelligent young man, and had received proper education from childhood. Furthermore, the sultan knew that his eldest son was generous with gold and money to the citizens he was governing, plus he was a fair decision-maker. In the year 1542, the Venetian ambassador Luigi Bassano wrote, "Mustafa founded another great court, now in the city of Amasya, and Mahidevran was his most trusted advisor."

In the year 1543, Prince Mehmet, the oldest son of Hurrem died of natural causes at the age of 22 years old; his death was unexpected and sudden. Prince Mehmet was said to be the favorite of Sultan Suleiman, and the one to assume the throne, however, this did not come to fruition. He is buried at *Prince's Mosque*, which is located on the opposite side of the street from the current day Istanbul Municipal building.

After the sudden death of Prince Mehmet, the Manisa governorship, the most important administration area did not stay vacant for a long time. At the surprise and disbelief again of Mahidevran and Mustafa, Prince Selim, the younger brother of deceased Mehmet was now appointed to govern this area. Meaning that Prince Mustafa was not the favorite of Sultan Suleiman for the throne; the throne was again closer to one of Hurrem's sons.

By 1546 two more of Suleiman's sons were ready to be governors, these were Beyazit and Cihangir. Therefore, the heavy and intense competition for succession continued among the princes.

Prince Beyazit was appointed to the governorship of the city of *Konya*, which is located in central Anatolia.

Prince Cihangir decided that he did not want to govern and stayed in the capital city of Istanbul, with his sultan father and mother Hurrem. Also, it should be written here now that Cihangir had a severe ailment from birth, he had a humped back that gave him severe pains. Plus, it was obvious from childhood that Cihangir was never a true contender for the throne.

Therefore, we can now summarize the princes who were candidates to the Ottoman throne, on the date of 1546, these were:
Mustafa - born in 1515, 31 years old, governor of Amasya,
Selim - born in 1524, 22 years old, governor of Manisa, and
Beyazit, born in 1525, 21 years old, governor of Konya.

Sultan Suleiman ruled for a very long 46 years, from the years 1520 to 1566, what is more, it was believed by the people, the time was long overdue for a successor. Particularly, the younger generation of the Ottomans wanted Mustafa to take the throne instead of his elderly father to continue to be the sultan.

As mentioned on several occasions, Prince Mustafa had grown extremely popular amongst the common people due to the generosity he lavished upon them and amongst the janissary soldiers that he led valiantly in many successful battles against neighboring countries, along-side his sultan father. Mustafa reminded the people of his grandfather Stern Sultan Selim, (the father of Suleiman), because he was fair, just, and firm. Mustafa was expected to succeed Suleiman even though there was no formal succession system put in place.

But the acceptance by most that Mustafa would succeed to the throne was unwelcomed by Hurrem because she knew this meant the death of her sons, and even the death of herself.

Nonetheless, was this the case? Would Prince Mustafa, upon ascending to the throne kill his younger siblings? The answer is a definite no. Mustafa did not show aggressive and violent postures towards his family, therefore, the sentence-layer will surmise to state that Mustafa would not have gone the path of killing his younger brothers, because, he valued and loved his siblings.

The rumors and speculations were heard clearly by everyone within the empire of the intense rivalry between the mothers of the remaining sons. Furthermore, there were false and bad rumors made about all princes that were mostly not taken seriously by the sultan father. However, the statement of *the tale grew as telling* was a perfect proclamation of the rumor about treason, which will be elaborated in detail in the next paragraph.

In the year 1553, Grand Vizier Rustem Pasha, who was Hurrem's daughter Mihrimah's husband, fuelled a false tale to Suleiman's ear of treason and disloyalty. The treason was said to be with the Persian Shah *Ismail* and his son, future Shah *Tahmasp*; Sultan Suleiman's worst nemeses. The false charge against the people's number one **hope** of the new heir was planning and organizing with the enemy to dethrone his sultan father. To this day, the charge of treason against Mustafa has neither been proven nor disproven.

The sentence-layer would like to assert that being objective and impartial is important while writing this story. Nevertheless, in the matter regarding this event that occurred almost 500 years ago, one cannot help but make the following statement, *Mustafa, did not dishonor his father, he did not betray him - he was loyal till the very end.*

In 1553, Ambassador Bernado Navagero wrote the following, "It is impossible to describe how much he (Mustafa) is loved and desired by all to succeed to the throne."

Prince Mustafa did not require alliances with any neighboring country or empire, especially a neighbor that was not liked by his father. Mustafa did not require help to ascend to the throne; he was much loved by the citizens within the empire and the janissary soldiers, which would have been enough for him to assume the throne. Therefore, the false accusation was very much obvious, but Sultan Suleiman did not recognize that the treason accusation was a fabricated action.

In the same year, Sultan Suleiman undertook a campaign against the *Safavid Dynasty* that was ruled by Persian Shah Ismail. Suleiman ordered his janissary army, which was stationed in *Uskudar* (a neighborhood on the Asian continent side of Istanbul) to march eastward to the borders of the empire. Suleiman accompanied his army to the town of *Eregli*, which was located in the district of Konya province of central Anatolia, and halted the army here for a well-needed break. Furthermore, the sultan had previously ordered his Grand Vizier Rustem Pasha to invite Mustafa to join him for the march and campaign to the eastern borders of the empire. There would be no campaigning to the eastern borders by father and son; this was a lie to lure Mustafa to join his sultan father.

The sultan's mind was made up, he was going to have his eldest son killed at this location due to the treason that his son had (supposedly) committed, which was voiced to him by Hurrem's son-in-law - the Grand Vizier of the Ottoman Empire, Rustem Pasha.

The mother of Mustafa - Mahidevran, who had maintained a network of informants in the capital city of Istanbul, heard that it was not ideal for her son to join Suleiman at the town of Eregli. Moreover, she was informed that there would be a plot to kill her son. The Republic of Venetia, nobleman, and ambassador *Do-*

menico Trevisano also confirmed that a warning message was sent from mother to son.

Mahidevran, who was not with Mustafa, as he had started his travel already, sent him a letter, warning him of what was to come if he was to meet his father. Mustafa received the letter from his mother the night before the meeting with his sultan father, as he was camped four kilometers away from Eregli, at the neighboring town named *Aktepe*. Mahidevran's heartbreaking letter was as follows:

"My love, my wealth, my one and only son Mustafa. You are my very existence and joy, I pray to the almighty that you receive this letter, and I pray to him again that you are alive, in good condition, and good health.

I have bad news to relay to you today, and I am confident that you will take my heed to heart, and listen to your mother, who values you, who loves you, like nothing else on this shameful world - a shameful world, where a father plots to kill his son.

Yes, you read that correctly. Please listen to your mother, my heart is aching in fear and worry at this moment. Please turn around immediately and ride back to your home, to your family, to your governorship home.

I received word from a reliable vizier at Topkapi Palace that on your meeting with your sultan father at Eregli, there will be a plot to kill you. I believe this to be a sincere and true warning, as your sultan father has not put together common sense to create a logical thought, since Hurrem entered his life, therefore, please listen to your mother, and DO NOT GO TO MEET YOUR FATHER.

I cannot bear to hear or see any harm come to you, just the thought of it has my hands and knees shaking. I am very much distressed currently, waiting impatiently to see you again.

Please, return home to us my springtime, my summer, my only happiness. May the almighty help all of us, but help you the most.

Your loving mother - Mahidevran,"

Mustafa read his mother's letter exactly three times, back-to-back, however, the sentence-layer is sad to write that the number one **hope** of the people for the change on the throne of the empire, ignored his mother's heartfelt warnings. Yes, Mustafa did not listen to his mother's warning.

The same evening, the evening before the meeting, there was a second warning message sent to Mustafa; to this day, it is not known who sent it. An arrow with a letter attached to it was shot at Mustafa's tent. In the letter, there was a message saying to not meet his sultan father, as there was talk of a plan to execute him. Mustafa ignored this anonymous warning as well. The anonymous letter reads as:

"Prince Mustafa, if you are reading this letter, you have received it, and I want you to take what is written in this letter as gravely serious.

I have to warn you that there is a plot to kill you tomorrow when you meet Sultan Suleiman. There is a charge of treason against you.

My advice to you is this, send a message to Sultan Suleiman tonight, tell him you have caught a very bad cold, and need to immediately return to your government building. He will believe this, and this will buy you time to investigate the treason charge against you.

Turn around and return to your governorship now. I have to keep my identity secret for the time being.

My prince, you are the one ruler, we the soldiers have, and we need you to stay alive, please take this warning seriously, please take it to heart. Sincerely,"

Mustafa read this second warning letter multiple times. But the number one contender to the throne, in the eyes of the people, ignored this second genuine and sincere warning letter as well.

Mustafa believed that he needed to meet his sultan father to explain that he had not betrayed him. Mustafa honestly assumed that if he had the opportunity to talk with his father, his father would believe his side of the story, and forgive him.

The next morning, on the date of October 6, 1553, he met his father as planned. Mahidevran and many others made great efforts to protect the chosen one from assassinations, but they could not prevent his eventual death, at the hands of Sultan Suleiman.

The Lawmaker was inside a make-shift large black-colored tent, in the early morning of the dreadful and infamous day of October sixth. He was sitting on a baldachin throne seat, made of walnut wood, waiting impatiently, for his eldest son to arrive for the planned meeting.

Mustafa arrived on horseback, he dismounted in front of the black as death-colored tent, walked to meet the high-ranking state officers, who were standing in front of the entrance. Mustafa's janissary elite protection of guards arrived with him, however stood three meters back, watching closely to the events that were unfolding in front of them. Their leader was getting reading to meet his father.

Mustafa was told to hand over his equipment of sword and knives, before entering the tent to meet his father; he did not object, even though this demand was never before made. The people's **hope** unhooked his one heavy metal sword passed it over, afterward he gave his two small knives to the state officers. He was now without protection.

Before entering the dark and shadowy large tent, Mustafa glanced back at his janissary elite protection of guards that were standing meters away and made a slow-motion with his head, a motion of nodding up and down, to mean, *just stay cool, I got this*. Plus, there was a nervous crooked smile on his face; overall, he was trying very hard to send the message to his small group of janissary elite guards, *stay calm, and wait for me to exit the black tent.*

Mustafa was not successful in calming his janissary elite guards, but they stayed put, and waited impatiently, irritably, and on edge.

The elite protection of guards watched as their leader, their **hope** entered the sultan's sinister black tent, this was the last time, they would see Mustafa alive.

Mahidevran tried to save her only grandson named Mehmet (Prince Mustafa's only son) as well, but she failed. Little Prince Mehmet was executed three days after Mustafa's execution, at just six years of age.

Why was Prince Mehmet executed? The reason was that Sultan Suleiman did not want him to revenge the death of his father - Mustafa, by coming after him one day.

After Mustafa's execution in the year 1553, Mahidevran lived a life as a recluse, she settled in the city of *Bursa*, where her son and grandson were buried. She died in 1581, outliving Suleiman and Hurrem, and she was buried in Mustafa's tomb.

CHAPTER FOUR

The family, friends, and rivals of Mustafa

"Those who make peaceful revolution impossible will make violent revolution inevitable." --- John Fitzgerald Kennedy

"I wish my eyes had not seen this event." --- Taslica Yahya (poem written for Mustafa)

"Fly away birds, fly to my birth place." --- Lyrics from the Turkish song titled, Fly away birds, song by Ahmet Kaya (writers - Riza Tevfik Bolukbasi and Ahmet Kaya)

Before writing further, in a future chapter, and giving a detailed account of what a deathly ordeal Mustafa, the chosen one, the **hope** of the people experienced while walking into his sultan father's black and shadowy large tent, let us write briefly about each of the main characters of this intriguing and fascinating large sultanate family members. The valued readers will remember most of the family members, however, there are a few that have been mentioned in only one or two lines, and a couple of them, have not been written about yet, here now, are the sultanate family members.

Lawmaker Sultan Suleiman (lived from: November 6, 1494, to September 6, 1566) (age of death: 72 years old)

The sentence-layer will not write in length about Suleiman in this chapter, as previously, many paragraphs of the merciless and heartless ruler have been written already, but a very brief synopsis is justifiable now.

He was the ruler of the Ottoman Empire from 1520 to 1566, a total of 46 very very long years on the throne. Suleiman was the longest-ruling sultan, among all the others in the 600 plus year history of the Ottomans.

He was born in the year 1494, by the southern shores of the Black Sea, in the city of Trabzon, and passed away unexpectedly during a wartime campaign against the Hungarian Empire, at the outskirts of the city of *Szigetvar,* a town in Baranya County in southern Hungary in the year 1566. Suleiman was 72 years old when he passed away, and he is resting at the *Suleimaniye Mosque* in Istanbul.

Thirteen years before his death, in the summer of 1553, Suleiman boarded his carriage, with the large Ottoman army around him, for a war campaign against the Safavid Empire. Before he departed from Istanbul for the slow track to the eastern borders of the empire, Suleiman sent a written order to Prince Mustafa to tell him to join this campaign against the *Safavids,* and to meet him at the town of Eregli, which was located at the outskirts of the city of Konya.

Despite the warnings from multiple individuals, particularly his mother Mahidevran, Mustafa decided to still join his father's army, stating to his advisors, "destiny sends me and I will go." Furthermore, if Sultan Suleiman sends a demand message to join him, how could Prince Mustafa refuse or reject this? He had to go.

On October 6, 1553, Mustafa arrived at his father's tent to kiss his hand.

This is where we will leave it for the time being, as the point of this section was to write a brief synopsis of Sultan Suleiman.

It was a well-known fact that Suleiman had his eldest son Mustafa killed for a treason charge that was never fully proven, even after 500 years have passed. The verdict cannot be made yet, the verdict of, *did Mustafa betray his sultan father?* This question is left for the readers to decide.

The story of the terrible incident, the death of Mustafa will be written without bias, just the bare facts.

The question must be on the readers' minds, "where will the tale of the sad death be written?" It will be written in complete detail, without holding anything back, in chapter six, please be patient, we are headed there, indeed.

Hurrem Haseki Sultan (lived from: 1502 or 1504 to April 15, 1558) (age of death: 53 to 56 years old)

Hurrem will not be written in length, in this chapter, as hitherto, she has been written about already, nevertheless, a summary is acceptable.

Hurrem was the wife of Suleiman, and the mother of the following children: Mehmet, Mihrimah, Selim, Beyazit, and Cihangir. Furthermore, Hurrem (repeating the meaning of the name one more time as it will beneficial - *one who is cheerful*) Haseki (meaning - *chief wife*) was the main rival of Mahidevran.

She was born in the year 1502 (or 1504, the actual date of birth is not known) in the province of *Ruthenia*, which was then part of the Polish Kingdom; now part of Ukraine. Hurrem passed away at the age of 53 (to 56, again, the actual age of death is not known) in the year 1558, at the capital city of Istanbul, she is buried alongside Suleiman, at the Suleimaniye Mosque.

Hurrem held an inordinate amount of power and influence from which everyone in the sultanate family was not safe from. Her fantastic and extraordinary rise and unachievable position for close to forty years caused many to believe that Hurrem was a crazy witch, who put a hypnotic spell on Lawmaker Sultan Suleiman.

Hurrem was very much loved and adored by the Lawmaker, and in the year 1554, one year after the death of Prince Mustafa, the Republic of Venetia, nobleman, and Ambassador *Domenico Tre-*

visano wrote about Sultan Suleiman and Hurrem's continued love affair as follows, "his majesty, the sultan loves Hurrem so much that as they say, he has refused to be with any other woman but her; none of his predecessors had ever done that and such a thing is unheard of among the Turks who have a custom of sleeping with many wives."

Hurrem died in 1558 and was buried in a domed mausoleum built by *Mimar Sinan Aga* (*Aga* meaning - *high ranking officer*), who was the Grandmaster architect of the empire. Sinan Aga decorated the mausoleum with elegant and delicate tiles from the city of *Iznik*. The tiles are depicting the *Garden of Paradise* in memory of her joyful and happy character that she outwardly acted, but witnessed only by Sultan Suleiman.

It was observed by everyone at the Topkapi Palace that Suleiman was so sad about the death of Hurrem that he did not regain happiness for the rest of his days. Eight long years later, in the year 1566, the aged sultan died while besieging the town of *Szigetvar* in Hungary. He was brought back to Istanbul and was laid to rest in a somber and dark mausoleum adjacent to that of his beloved Hurrem, located in the courtyard of the Suleimaniye Mosque.

Similar to Suleiman, a lengthy telling about Hurrem was not completed. This is where we will leave it, as the point of this section was to write a summary.

There was no concrete proof of Hurrem's direct involvement in her stepson's death. Nevertheless, plenty of rumors indicated that she was continually plotting against Mustafa to eliminate him, ensuring that one of her sons made it to the power seat - the throne of the mighty empire.

Mahidevran Gulbahar Sultan (lived from: 1500 to February 3, 1581) (age of death: 81 years old)

She was the companion of Suleiman when he was a young man, a young prince at the city of Manisa. Mahidevran (meaning - *one who is beautiful* or *one whose beauty never fades*) Gulbahar (meaning - *rose spring*) was the mother of Mustafa.

She was born in the year 1500, however, her birth location, background, and ethnicity are a matter of debate still. Sadly, we cannot write in concrete terms where the mother of Mustafa was originally from, we can only give an idea of where she might be from.

It is accepted now and narrowed to two locations; she is either *Albanian* or *Circassian*. The interesting dilemma is that these two locations are of exact opposite areas of the empire.

Therefore, why do historians narrow her ethnicity to these two regions? The answer is that in the Ottoman Empire, during Sultan Suleiman's rule, there were many transactions with these two neighbors. The Ottomans had the most dealings with both the Albanians and Circassians, out of all other neighboring countries. Furthermore, the sultan's harem welcomed young maidens from the neighboring countries, particularly from these two regions.

Little to nothing about her early life is known. But, we do know an important fact about her; we know that she entered into the harem of Prince Suleiman in the city of Manisa, at the age of 15.

After the death of her son Mustafa, Mahidevran had a difficult life for several years. Mustafa's body was sent away to *Bursa* to be buried, far away from the capital city of Istanbul. She followed her son's corpse to this city and took control of the burial and spent her entire fortune on the building and upkeep of Mustafa's tomb.

She retired in this city, but her finances suffered horribly as Sultan Suleiman stopped sending her a salary, the salary of being the mother of a prince as, after the death of Mustafa, she was no longer that. Mahidevran was unable to pay the rent on the house in which she lived; she was in desperate financial hardship during these years.

Mahidevran's situation improved after Sultan Suleiman's reign ended, and her debts were paid and the house she was living in was purchased for her. It is widely believed by historians that these kindnesses were completed by Mustafa's half-brother - Selim II.

Mahidevran passed away in the year 1581 in Bursa, which was the old capital city of the empire; she was 81 years old at the time of her death. She is buried next to her son Mustafa at *Muradiye Complex*, located at *Muradiye* neighborhood, within the town of *Osmangazi*, located at the outskirts of Bursa.

Likewise, to Suleiman and Hurrem, Mahidevran will not be examined in this chapter directly, as the sentence-layer tried very hard to complete a factual, convincing, and lengthy portrayal of her earlier, in chapter number three. The portrayal of Mahidevran should be satisfactory for the readers.

Mahidevran's only son, the people's favorite prince, the number one contender to the throne, was brutally murdered by her old companion - Suleiman, this is an undeniable fact.

Prince Mehmet, son of Hurrem Sultan (lived from: *October 31, 1522, to November 7, 1543) (age of death: 21 years old)*

Now, here is a prince that has not been written about yet, just mentioned briefly in a paragraph or two previously.

Prince Mehmet was born in the year 1522; exactly two years after Suleiman became the ruler of the empire. He was the oldest child of Suleiman and Hurrem. Mehmet's birth changed the dynamics within the sultanate, as Mustafa was the only prince, until Mehmet was born. With Mehmet's arrival, the competition for the next ruler of the empire officially began.

Unlike the other children of Hurrem, which all had light features, Mehmet surprisingly had dark highlights. This was rather unique since both Suleiman and Hurrem were very much light-skinned. Mehmet had dark brown eyes and dark brown, almost black hair, with a light brown skin tone. Historians write that Mehmet resembled the features of the conqueror of *Istanbul*, his great grandfather, Conqueror Sultan Mehmet II, as the readers have surely noticed, the great grandfather's name was also Mehmet.

The prince was an intelligent and clever young man that had good judgment, stern character, and was a natural problem solver. It was evidenced that Suleiman favored Mehmet to the throne, as Mehmet was the son of his wife - Hurrem. Plus, when Mehmet became old enough to govern, he was given the city of Manisa; the readers should remember that this city was always given to the prince, who was favored to succeed to the throne. Furthermore, the governorship of Manisa was taken away from Mustafa and given to Mehmet; this action alone explained how much the younger prince was valued.

Mehmet passed away unexpectedly in the year 1443, in the city of Manisa; he was only 21 years old. It is said that he caught an infectious disease, and died within a very short period of time. Some historians believe that Mehmet died due to catching smallpox. Another strong opinion of his death was believed to be that he was poisoned, to make way for Mustafa to the throne. To this day, the latter opinion of poisoning is neither proven nor disproven, nonetheless, the death of Mehmet was rather unexpected, unfortunate, and tragic.

After his son's untimely death, Suleiman had the well-known regal architect, the grandest of architects of the empire - Mimar Sinan Aga build the Prince's Mosque in Istanbul to remember and celebrate Mehmet's young life. Suleiman was constructing the mosque already for himself, however, after his beloved son's untimely death, the commission of the mosque was altered. The modification of the mosque was made to show his love and affection for Mehmet, plus the mosque was named after him, his eldest son from Hurrem.

Similar to previous portrayals above, a lengthy telling about Mehmet will not be completed. This is where we will leave it, as the point of this section was to write a brief synopsis.

Mehmet had no involvement with the death of Mustafa since he passed away in the year 1543, which was exactly 10 years before Mustafa's execution, in the infamous year of 1553.

Mihrimah Sultan, daughter of Hurrem Sultan (lived from: 1523 to January 25, 1578) (age of death: 55 years old)

Here is another important individual from the sultanate family that has not been written about in length yet, just mentioned briefly in a few paragraphs in chapter three.

This beautiful Ottoman princess was born in the year 1523, and she was the second child, the daughter of the power couple - Hurrem and Suleiman. After her mother, Mihrimah become the most powerful imperial princess and woman during her father's rule.

Italian painter named *Cristofano dell'Altissimo*, from the city of *Florence* was invited to the capital city of the Ottoman Empire to paint a portrait of Mihrimah titled, *Cameria Solimani*. The title was in Italian to mean *Cameria Suleiman*, as Mihrimah was known as Cameria in the western world. The portrait is now located at Topkapi Palace, and it clearly showed how delicate, graceful, and striking the princess was. Similar to her parents, she had light features and a light skin tone.

In the year 1539, at the age of 17, Mihrimah married *Rustem Pasha*, who at the time was the governor of the far east city of *Diyarbakir*. After five years, in the year 1544, her husband Rustem became the authoritative grand vizier to his father-in-law - Sultan Suleiman. Therefore, the young powerful couple became extremely controlling in the political affairs within the empire and were very much influential in the decisions made by and with their father - Suleiman.

Furthermore, she traveled throughout the empire, alongside her husband and father, during peace and wartime campaigns. Mihrimah became Suleiman's confidant, consultant, and closest living relative, after the sultan's other relatives and companions died, executed, or were exiled one after the other. After Hurrem's death, this was even more prevalent, Mihrimah took her mother's place as her father's sole advisor, urging him to undertake the conquests and campaigns on neighboring lands, and sent him news from the Topkapi Palace, while he was absent from the capital. An example of her urging and encouragement was when she funded the building of 400 warships at her own expense for her sultan father, for the difficult and blood-soaked campaign against the island of *Malta*.

Besides her great political intelligence, Mihrimah also had access to considerable resources and funded many architectural projects throughout the empire. Examples of her funding projects include two mosques that bear her name, both designed by her father's chief architect of Sinan Aga.

The first mosque complex that bears her name is *Mihrimah Sultan Mosque*, which is located in the neighborhood named Uskudar of Istanbul, and built between the years 1546 to 1548.

The second mosque is also named Mihrimah Sultan Mosque, but this one is located in the neighborhood called *Edirne Kapi* (meaning - *Adrianople Gate*), at the western walled area of the European side of Istanbul. This mosque was completed between the years 1562 to 1565.

As the years rolled by, Mihrimah was caught-up in the whirlwind of the conflicts and back-room-deals for the next ruler of the empire. Like many, she was also cheering for her favorite race-horse (brother) to ascend to the throne. It was believed that out of all of her full brothers (Cihangir, Beyazit, and Selim), Mihrimah favored her middle brother Beyazit to the throne, instead of Selim, the older one. She supported Beyazit openly with financial favors.

However, she was not favoring Mustafa to be the next ruler, and therefore would easily give-up on Beyazit, if the choices were between either Selim or Mustafa. Mihrimah would rather have Selim sit on the throne of the empire, instead of her half-brother Mustafa.

Mihrimah died in the year 1578, at the age of 55 years old. She was buried next to her parents of Hurrem and Suleiman, at the mosque that bears her sultan father's name of Suleimaniye Mosque. Interestingly, Mihrimah is the only one of Hurrem and Suleiman's children that were buried next to them.

This is where we will leave it, similar to previous portrayals above, only a brief synopsis was written.

There is no concrete proof of Mihrimah's direct involvement in her half-brother Mustafa's death. However, plenty of rumors and sources indicate that it was widely believed Mihrimah, along with her mother Hurrem, and her husband Rustem, worked closely to eliminate and remove Mustafa; consequently, ensuring the Ottoman throne to one of her full brothers.

Grand Vizier Rustem Pasha, husband of Mihrimah Sultan, (lived from: 1500 to July 10, 1561) (Age of death: 61 years old)

Here is the husband of Mihrimah, another central figure from the sultanate family, who has not been written about yet.

Mihrimah's husband was *Rustem Pasha*, who was born in the year 1500 as a Christian. He was born just outside the borders of the empire, in the county of *Croatia*, which would soon become a province of the Ottomans, in the year 1526, with the loss of the *Battle of Mohacs*.

He converted to the religion of Islam upon being delivered to the Topkapi Palace. Rustem was brought into the *janissary* soldier system as a child and rose gradually among the soldier ranks.

Young Rustem studied at a special janissary barracks, which was a private, multicultural boarding school for children that were brought from different locations and corners of the empire. The graduates of these private schools were able to speak, read, and write at least three different languages. The favorite languages thought were: Ottoman Turkish, Persian, Arabic, and Latin. Furthermore, the students were able to understand the latest developments in science, finance, and the economy. The brightest and intelligent of the students were encouraged and demanded to pursue further education and learning while climbing to higher janissary positions; some made it into the close-knit bureaucratic line of the empire.

Rustem, similarly to some other Christian boys was captured from outside the borders of the empire. He was taken as a child, to serve at the Topkapi Palace, and it was here that he built a brilliant and exceptional military career. He rose among the janissary ranks, and eventually became the governor of the faraway city of Diyarbakir; it was during this duty that he caught the eye of Suleiman. Rustem was an unbiased and fair governor, with a touch of malevolent character that he subdued when required.

This well-educated young man rose to the very zenith of the empire; he married the daughter of Suleiman, in the year 1539, when he was 39 years old, and Mihrimah being only 17 years of age. Furthermore, he was shown much love within the sultanate family, since he was referred to as *Damat* (meaning - *son-in-law*) Rustem Pasha.

Additionally, Rustem became the Grand Vizier to Suleiman in the year 1544, at the young age of 43 years old. Ultimately, Rustem was going to be known as one of the most powerful and successful Grand Viziers of the Ottoman Empire; this was a great achievement as there were many influential viziers throughout the 600 plus years of the empire. Finally, he became the wealthiest grand vizier in the history of the empire; this was a rather impressive career and life of a Christian pig farmer's son.

While being the grand vizier, Rustem initiated many trade agreements with western European powers. One of his biggest successes in the diplomatic area was the agreement signed in the year 1547 with *Emperor Ferdinand I* of the Holy Roman Empire and the *Emperor Charles V* of the Spanish Empire. With these agreements, and without even firing a single canon, the western borders of the Ottoman Empire were secure and peaceful for more than 20 consecutive years. Ferdinand and Charles agreed to each pay a tax of 30,000 gold ducats per year into the Ottoman treasury.

Jean Chesneau wrote about Rustem Pasha with kind sentiments, "the grand vizier is a man of humble origin, who, thanks to his talent and will, worked his way up from nothing." He went on to write, "Rustem is an agreeable companion, engaging your interest with his acute faculty of judgment, and insightful way of thinking and magnanimous manners. During the negotiations, he is calm and dispassionate, although in his views determined."

On top of his political success, Rustem also funded many architectural projects throughout the empire. One example of his funding project was the *Rustem Pasha Mosque*, which is located in the *Eminonu* neighborhood of Istanbul. The mosque was also designed and built by the famous imperial architect of Sinan Aga. The mosque was built between the years 1561 to 1563.

The relationship between his wife Mihrimah did not bring about flowery love letters and poems written for one another, as Hurrem and Suleiman, their parent's extensive productions to each other. But Mihrimah was a dedicated and loyal wife, who was always by her husband's side and aide. After his death in the year 1561, she posthumously finished the Rustem Pasha Mosque, since Rustem died a few months after the project started. The Rustem Pasha Mosque is one of Sinan Aga's most impressive and notable projects, the sentence-layer has been inside this mosque and can vouch wholeheartedly.

Rustem died in the year 1561, after suffering a long illness of *hydrocephalus* (meaning - *abnormal water build-up in the brain*). Due to his untimely passing, he was buried at the Prince's Mosque, next to Suleiman's son of Prince Mehmet, instead of his mosque, since it was not ready.

This is a good summary of Rustem Pasha, and the sentence-layer will stop here, similar to previous portrayals, only a brief synopsis was written. However, Rustem will be written further in chapter five, while Mustafa's life and struggles are detailed.

There are various versions of reports on Mustafa's sad and untimely end at the town of Eregli. According to one version, Rustem made an offer to Mustafa to join his sultan father's army for the previously planned march against the Safavid Dynasty, and at the same time, he warned Suleiman that Mustafa was coming with his army to fight against him, kill him, and finally to take over the Ottoman throne.

According to another version, it was Suleiman himself who summoned his son to confront him of treason charges, which were whispered to the sultan's ear distastefully and eagerly by Rustem. Along with the whispering, there were letters produced and accompanied, and given to the sultan, which contained Mustafa's (fake) signatures, and lengthy communications with neighboring empires for the dethroning of Sultan Suleiman.

It is believed that Hurrem and her persuasive only daughter Mihrimah, plus her son-in-law, the highly dominant Grand Vizier Rustem Pasha conspired strongly against Mustafa for many years. In all versions of the reports, one of the three mentioned conspirators is always stated as a ruthless antagonist.

Prince Cihangir, son of Hurrem Sultan (lived from: December 9, 1531, to November 27, 1553) (age of death: 22 years old)

Another crucial and important figure from the Ottoman family, who has not been written about yet.

Prince Cihangir (meaning - *World conqueror*) was the youngest child of Sultan Suleiman and his wife Hurrem Sultan. Cihangir, from birth, had multiple health problems, plus, he was born with a noticeable humped back, which got bigger as he grew older. Due to his humped back, he stayed in his home for the majority of the time, out of sight from almost everyone, and mostly read, consequently, he was the smartest and brightest of his siblings.

Further to the humped back, Cihangir had an aching spinal curvature in the upper part of his body, plus, his one shoulder was unusually higher than the other. Moreover, as the youngest child in the family and as a result of his severe disability, Cihangir was loved and treated with gentle love by everyone.

Cihangir was very well educated and wrote poems with the pen name *Zarifi* (meaning - *elegant one*), furthermore, he was also interested in calligraphy writing.

Cihangir was not sent to a provincial governorship duty, since he did not see himself to be the next ruler of the empire. Cihangir voluntarily resigned from the rat race to the throne, he had said to his sultan father, "I'm not interested in the throne of the empire."

Therefore, Cihangir lived in the Topkapi Palace all his life except for two long periods, when he left his home, these were:
The second Iran expedition in the year 1548, and
The third Iran expedition in 1553, which he did not return alive from.

In the third Iran expedition, Cihangir together with his father, Sultan Suleiman departed from Istanbul and reached the plains of Eregli. Eregli was the predetermined location to meet with janissaries from different parts of the empire, before heading to the eastern borders for Iran. At this location, Cihangir was to also meet his older half-brother Mustafa, but the meeting did not happen, since Mustafa was strangled by Sultan Suleiman's guards, in the sultan's black tent.

Cihangir did not witness this horrible strangulation of this older brother, as he was sent out on a hunting expedition, however, on his return, he heard of the awful event and had a nervous breakdown, but fortunately survived. However, his condition did not fully improve, and when the Ottoman army arrived in the city of *Aleppo*, Cihangir's frail condition worsened.

Prince Cihangir was extremely weak and unhappy throughout the journey from Eregli to Aleppo, and could not tolerate the horrendous event that bestowed onto his older brother, plus the difficult journey drained his frail and weak body. Sadly, he passed away at the young age of 22 in Aleppo.

The body of Cihangir was sent from Aleppo to Istanbul, and he was buried in the tomb of his deceased older brother Prince Mehmet. Do the readers remember where Prince Mehmet is buried?

Sultan Suleiman had Mimar Sinan Aga build the Prince's Mosque in Istanbul to remember and celebrate his son Mehmet's young life. Cihangir is now buried in the same tomb as his older brother, and only 10 years after the death of Mehmet (date of death 1443), Cihangir joined his older brother (death of death 1553), both were untimely and tragic deaths.

The Istanbul neighborhood on the European side is named Cihangir after Prince Cihangir, when his father had a modest wooden mosque built in this area, overlooking the *Bosphorus* (meaning - *waterway*) to remember his death.

Based on our current knowledge, the reported findings indicate that Cihangir was suffering from *spinal dysraphism*, which is an umbrella term that describes several conditions present at birth that affect the spine, spinal cord, or nerve roots.

Thus, Cihangir was born with a spinal dysraphism, with extreme neurological complications, right from his birth to the day he passed away. Furthermore, he went on long military expeditions on horseback, which deteriorated his already weakened condition.

On the other hand, it is also reported that Cihangir was going through deep sorrow after the news of the murder of his older brother of Mustafa. It is a strong possibility that Cihangir was deeply depressed at the loss of Mustafa, and suffered a psychological major depression that resulted in his death.

This is where we will leave it, as the point of this section was to write a summary. But obviously, the reader's surely have noticed, the sentence-layer does not know yet, how to be brief, plus he rather enjoyed researching and writing about Prince Cihangir, and could not stop himself from detailing the young prince's life, nevertheless, let us stop here now.

Cihangir had no involvement with the death of Mustafa, and there is a strong argument that Cihangir died of the sorrow of knowing his older brother was murdered by his sultan father. Cihangir had an extreme problem knowing that his father could commit such an act, this hurt him greatly.

The year 1553 saw two sons of Sultan Suleiman tragically pass away. This year marked a great sadness in the Ottoman Empire.

Prince Beyazit, son of Hurrem (lived from: 1525 to September 25, 1561) (age of death: 31 years old)

Another strong character from the Ottoman family, who has not been written about yet, just mentioned in brief previously.

Prince Beyazit was the son of the power couple of Sultan Suleiman and his wife Hurrem. Beyazit was born in the year 1525, at the Topkapi Palace, during the reign of his sultan father. Beyazit had the following full and half brothers, these were:
Mustafa (born 1515) (half brother),
Mehmet (born 1521) (full brother),
Abdullah (born 1522) (full brother, died of natural causes a few years after his birth),
Selim (born 1524) (full brother), and
Cihangir (born 1531) (full brother).

Beyazit became the governor of the western Anatolian city of *Kutahya* for several years, starting from his late teens, however, during his sultan father's campaign against the *Safavid Empire* in 1553, he was appointed to rule in Edirne, which was the second capital of the empire. Edirne is only 240 kilometers away from the capital city of Istanbul.

The readers should know by now that during the campaign against the Safavid's, Prince Mustafa was executed, and the unhappy news of the execution reached all corners of the empire, and Beyazit was very much saddened by the news. He was ready to ride to Istanbul, to take over the throne, in the absence of his sultan father, who was located in the town of Eregli. Nonetheless, Beyazit was subdued by his advisors, and he was told to be patient, as surely, the throne would be his eventually, now that Prince Mustafa was murdered.

An impostor within Beyazit's advisors reached the news to Sultan Suleiman, who never forgave his son for even thinking of wanting to take over the throne by force from him.

As stated numerous times thus far, Prince Mustafa was the heir apparent to the illustrious throne of the mighty empire, however, after his hasty execution in the year 1553, Beyazit became the popular choice among the people and the janissaries, to be the next heir, instead of his older brother Selim. Beyazit resembled Mustafa in character and personality, therefore, the people came to favor him.

After Mustafa's execution, the two remaining princes, Selim and Beyazit, entered into a heated race for the throne, since Suleiman was in his 60s and everyone was assuming it would be any day that the throne would see a change. Suleiman scolded both of his sons for their childish actions and changed their *provincial government locations*, to have both of them further away from Istanbul; Beyazit was assigned to rule *Amasya* and Selim to *Konya*.

However, at the tail end of the decade, Beyazit fell into disfavor with his sultan father, due to his disobedience and rebellion. The two brothers finally met on the battlefield in the year 1559, with Sultan Suleiman siding with Selim, and allowing him to command the Ottoman army against Beyazit's smaller army.

At the defeat of this battle, Beyazit took his family and fled to the eastern borders of the empire, to the neighbor of the Safavid Empire, where he was extravagantly received by the sultan of the Safavid's, the ruthless *Tahmasp*. Although Tahmasp initially enthusiastically welcomed Beyazit, including giving magnificent dinners and parties in the prince's honor, he later understood that holding the prince would bring about another war, as Sultan Suleiman would surely attack.

In the year 1561, after two years of living with his family in an open prison, Beyazit was handed over to Sultan Suleiman's men, in exchange for a large sum of gold and Ottoman land, precisely the eastern portion of the Province of *Van*.

Beyazit and his entire family (sons) were executed on the return home to Istanbul, the family is buried in the city of *Sivas*. Do the readers want to know who were all cruelly and coldly executed? Here below are all of the sons of Beyazit executed on September 25, 1561:
Orhan (born 1543, age at execution 18),
Osman (born 1545, age at execution 16),
Abdullah (born 1548, age at execution 13),
Mahmud (born 1552, age at execution 9), and
Mehmet (born 1559, age at execution 2).

Looking at the names above, the readers will feel incredible sadness and trouble by the execution. Yes, it was unreal, but it did happen.

This is where we will leave it, as the point of this section was to write a summary.

Undoubtedly, Beyazit did not have any involvement with the death of Mustafa, and additionally, there is a convincing agreement that he was much upset at his sultan father for murdering his older brother, so much so that, Beyazit almost rode to Istanbul to take the Ottoman throne forcibly.

Sultan Selim II, son of Hurrem (lived from: May 28, 1524 to December 15, 1574) (age of death: 50 years old)

The future sultan of the empire, Selim, who was an important character from the Ottoman dynasty has not been written about yet, just mentioned briefly before.

Selim was born in Istanbul on May 28, 1524, during the reign of his sultan father. He became the ruler of the Ottoman Empire on September 7, 1566, when his father died during the seize of *Sziget-var* in Hungary. He was the ruler of the Ottoman Empire from 1566 to 1574, a total of 12 years. Selim was also known as *Selim the Blond* or *Selim the Drunk*. He was the first sultan to be born in Istanbul, all prior sultans were born in either Edirne, Bursa, Trabzon, or other locations in Anatolia.

In 1545, at the age of 21, Selim married *Nurbanu Sultan*, in the city of Konya. The couple's firstborn was *Murat III*, who would be the successor to the Ottoman throne, in the year 1574.

Selim was an implausible and doubtful candidate to the throne of the empire, but the other candidates, namely his brothers all died or murdered, his brothers and causes of death were:
Mehmet, his full brother, died of smallpox on November 7, 1543,
Mustafa, his half brother was strangled to death by the order of their sultan father on October 5, 1553,
Cihangir, his full brother died of grief at the news of Mustafa's execution on November 27, 1553, and
Beyazit, his full brother was killed on the order of their sultan father, after a rebellion against him on September 25, 1561.

Yes, as written previously, Selim was an implausible candidate to the throne, but the below conversation showed how clever, enduring, and expressive he was. The following discussion occurred, while Selim was still a prince at his governorship palace in Manisa. One night, while he was with his advisors, one of them, his name being *Celal Bey*, said the following in regards to who would be the next sultan, after Lawmaker Sultan Suleiman, "The janissaries want Mustafa, Hurrem, your mother wants Beyazit, Suleiman, your father wants Mehmet, what do you think about this?" The answer given by Selim was exceptionally poetic, the response back by the future sultan was, "Yes, I hear the rumors as well. Let them all make plans, but God plans the best, and here is trusting the almighty plans for me to be the next sultan. Let us enjoy ourselves." When he had said, "Here is trusting the almighty plans for me," Selim had raised his glass, which was half full with red wine from Cyprus, for a toast with Celal Bey.

During the rule of Sultan Suleiman, his father, the empire had grown rapidly, but Selim lacked the skills to maintain this growth and progress. Ruling the empire did not excite him, and he had handed over the power to his *Grand Vizier, Sokullu Mehmet Pasha* since Selim choose to be entertained and to stay out of the public's eye. Ottoman historians agree that the empire began the slow descent into becoming the *Sick man of Europe*, during the rule of Selim.

However, Selim was much generous as it was he who helped his half-brother Mustafa's mother by buying her the home she lived in. After becoming the sultan, he also assisted the building of the tomb of Mustafa by giving generously to fund it.

Again, let us be brief, and therefore, we will end it here, as the point of this section was to write a summary.

Selim gained greatly from all of the intrigue and battle in Topkapi Palace since every other heir apparent were brutally murdered or died. His mother Hurrem and her persuasive only daughter Mihrimah, plus, the intimidating Grand Vizier Rustem Pasha conspired against Mustafa for many years, at the benefit of Selim.

Grand Vizier Pargali Ibrahim Pasha (lived from: 1495 to March 15, 1536) (age of death: 41 years old)

Ibrahim Pasha was a loyal friend to Sultan Suleiman, until Hurrem came into the picture, furthermore, he was another important personality, but has not been written about much.

Ibrahim Pasha was born in the town of Parga, located in current-day Greece, but back in 1495, this area was inside the borders of the Republic of Venice, and soon after, would be incorporated into the Ottoman Empire. Consequently, Ibrahim was commonly known as *Pargali*, (the li meaning from), *Ibrahim Pasha from Parga*, but there were other names given to him, these were:
Frank Ibrahim Pasha (the one who is a westerner),
Makbul Ibrahim Pasha (the one who is the favorite), and
Maktul Ibrahim Pasha (the one who was executed).

Ibrahim was born to Orthodox Christian parents in Parga but spoke a Slavic dialect common to the *Ionian Sea* area. Ibrahim Pasha's story is very similar to Rustem Pasha's, in that, they were both Christian boys who were taken into the Ottoman janissaries at a very early age. Ibrahim entered the service of Sultan Suleiman, when he was still just a prince, governing the city of Manisa.

Under the service of Suleiman, Ibrahim rose very quickly and even reached the highpoint of power within the empire by becoming a grand vizier in 1523, when he was only 28 years old. He attained a level of authority and influence rivaled by only a handful of other grand viziers.

As the grand vizier, his negotiating against the neighbors of the empire was an absolute success, plus, he portrayed himself as the true power of the empire. The Venetian diplomats even referred to him as *Ibrahim the Magnificent*, which meant that he too was magnificent, maybe more so, or the true ruler, instead of Suleiman.

An example of his negotiating skills was in the year 1533 when he convinced *Charles V*, the ruler of the *Hungarian Empire* to turn into a vassal state for the Ottoman Empire.

As his power and wealth grew substantially, some believed so did his arrogance, and he continued to behave as if he was the true leader, the real ruler, not Suleiman. The supposed arrogance of *Ibrahim Pasha* troubled *Hurrem Sultan*, the two, by the way, never liked one another, and Hurrem started the plot of the pasha's downfall.

On March 5, 1536, a private dinner was held between Ibrahim Pasha and Sultan Suleiman, of which the grand vizier of the empire would not see the morning, since he was strangled by Suleiman's men.

What was Ibrahim Pasha's charge? It was believed and told to Suleiman that his best friend and confidant for a quarter of a century was plotting to take over the throne, which was indeed a false charge.

Another reason, surely the stronger reason was this, Ibrahim Pasha was plotted and murdered because he was a strong supporter of Prince Mustafa. Ibrahim was very close friends with Mustafa, as he almost raised him alongside Suleiman, and this close relationship troubled Hurrem. Having the grand vizier of the empire openly support Mustafa, more so than, the other princes (her sons) was not to be a good outcome in the coming years for Hurrem.

The elimination of Ibrahim Pasha put a caveat on Mustafa's path to the throne, plus, the throne was no longer a sure-shot for him, and he would need to work very hard to attain it, as others were wanting it very much in desperation.

The sentence-layer could write in length about Ibrahim Pasha, however, this would drive the story in another direction. Let us be brief, consequently, end it here, as the point of this section was to keep it short.

Ibrahim Pasha had no involvement with the death of Mustafa since he passed away in 1536, which was exactly seventeen years before Mustafa's execution, in the unforgettable year of 1553. But Ibrahim was an important figure in the Ottoman family dynamics. The close relationship Ibrahim had with Mustafa brought an end to his own life, furthermore, the strongest reason Mustafa lost the Ottoman throne was with the passing of Ibrahim since he was Mustafa's close friend; almost a second father.

Zal Mahmud Pasha (lived from: 1520 to 1580) (age of death: 60 years old)

Zal Mahmud Pasha has not been written about yet, not even mentioned in previous chapters. He is a very important figure since it was he who strangled the heir apparent to the throne.

Zal Mahmud (Mahmud meaning - *Praise*) became infamous in the notorious year of 1553; he was the pasha who strangled Mustafa to death, after the wrestling match that Mustafa had with six other soldiers, in the sultan's black colored tent.

Zal Mahmud was born in *Bosnia and Herzegovina* and his story is similar to both Pargali Ibrahim and Rustem since they were all Christian boys, who were taken into the Ottoman janissaries at a very early age. Zal Mahmud, like the other pasha's mentioned, was educated and served in the janissary army, and rose quickly, to become a soldier in Suleiman's elite guard unit.

Zal Mahmud Pasha was nicknamed *Zal* after the legendary hero of the *Shahnameh* (meaning - *The book of Kings*) long epic poem written by the Persian poet *Ferdowsi* in the year 977 that was the classic telling of Greater Iran. Both Zal from the poem and Mahmud were great wrestlers, therefore, the nickname Zal given to the Ottoman pasha.

Zal performed various bureaucratic positions and was appointed *Governor General* of Anatolia in 1564 and finally raised to the rank of *vizier* in 1567, under *Sultan Selim II's* rule.

He went on to marry *Sultan Selim II's* daughter, *Sah Sultan* in 1574, but Zal died a short six years after the marriage. However, before his death, Zal paid for the construction of the *Zal Mahmud Pasha Mosque*, located in the *Eyup* district of Istanbul. The pasha's well-designed tomb is located in the garden of this not-very-well-at-tended mosque.

As written many times, the common people loved Mustafa, he was their number one **hope** as the ruler, after the death of Sultan Suleiman. The love the people had for Mustafa, got to a legendary level, after the prince's death, since the common people did not forget him, but desired for him more, and compared all future sultan's to him.

When Zal Mahmud began the construction of his famous mosque with the same name as himself, in the year 1577, it had already been twenty-four years since Mustafa passed away to the ever-after. The mosque was completed thirteen years later, in 1590, the pasha had been dead for ten years already, and Mustafa was dead for a total of thirty-seven very very long years, please let those numbers sink in for a minute.

Zal Mahmud was dead for 10 years.

Prince Mustafa had passed away 37 years prior.

Now read the below paragraph to understand the love the common people had for Mustafa.

The people of the Eyup district of Istanbul did not attend the Zal Mahmud Pasha Mosque, due to the pasha having a heavy hand in the death of Mustafa. The imams who were assigned for duty at this mosque always complained and murmured about the low attendance in the mosque, while the neighboring mosques were jammed packed during prayer time.

Mustafa did leave a lasting positive impression on the common people.

Again, let us be brief, and therefore, we will end it here, as the point of this section was to write a summary. However, Zal Mahmud will come back into the story in chapter six, when Mustafa enters into the deadly big black tent of the sultan's.

Strangulation was the preferred choice to kill a person from the Ottoman dynasty, due to a policy to not spill blood when killing a member. Mustafa was wrestled down by half a dozen janissary soldiers, while Zal Mahmud strangled him with a thin white rope. Therefore, on the orders of Sultan Suleiman, Zal Mahmud killed Prince Mustafa.

Taslica Yahya Bey (lived from:1498 to 1582) (age of death: 84 years old)

Taslica Yahya Bey was an important Ottoman poet that has not been written about thus far, not even mentioned in previous chapters.

Taslica Yahya Bey was an Ottoman poet and military man, who was also known as _Taslica Bey Dukagjini_. He was of Albanian origin and wrote his famous poems in Ottoman Turkish.

Yahya was born in 1498 in what was known as _Taslica_ when the area was inside the borders of the Ottoman Empire, currently, _Taslica_ is the modern-day city of _Pljevlja_ of _Montenegro_. Therefore, Yahya was named _Taslica_ or _Taslicali_, meaning from Taslica.

Similar to the other pasha's written about already (Zal Mahmud, Pargali Ibrahim, and Rustem), Yahya was recruited at an early age, and taken into the Ottoman janissaries to be trained and educated as a soldier.

Yahya took part in many campaigns in his youth, including the _Battle of Chaldiran_ of August 23, 1514, led by _Sultan Selim I_ (Suleiman's father), Ottoman–Mamluk War of 1516, and the Baghdad mission of 1535 under Sultan Suleiman. He earned the respect of the viziers because of his poetry and military talent.

After the death of Mustafa, Yahya wrote an elegy named _Prince's Requiem_, which was well received by the Ottoman public. Nonetheless, the instigators behind the murder of Mustafa: Rustem Pasha, Hurrem Sultan, and Mihrimah Sultan (and a few others) were not happy about the elegy.

The Grand Vizier of the Ottoman Empire, Rustem Pasha summoned Yahya for a private meeting and demanded to know how he could grieve one, whom the sultan had condemned. Yahya responded, "we indeed condemned him with the sultan, but we grieved him along with the people." Here below is the tragic elegy, translated to English:
"Help, help, one side of the world has been devastated,
Angel of death took Sultan Mustafa.

The sun of his beauty set, his council dissolved,
With deceit, they made the family of Ottoman, carry this horrible moment.

They were bad-mouthing him when others mentioned that bravest man,
Fate turned the sultan of the world to their side.

The slander of the lie and his hidden grudge,
Made us shed tears, and lighted the fire of separation.

He didn't murder anyone as they murdered in blood,
He got drowned in the flood of disaster, his men disbanded.

I wish my eyes had not seen this event,
Despaired we were, this judgment was not fit for him.

He got decorated with whites like a minaret lighted at night,
He was genuine like the morning.

He appeared to the people, like a tree in a flower garden,
He walked among his people like a tulip garden.

Sultan of the world was standing with anger, like fire,
His black tent was like snowy mountain tops.

The tent was decorated with bodies like a white fortress,
He walked towards the unstable sun to kiss his hand.

He didn't come back, because he turned into an eclipsed moon,

People who had seen this cried like spring clouds.

This black tent of the world was like a two-headed dragon,
One who falls into the mouth disappears.

That dragon brought the backside of time,
The harm came to his body from the cruelty of Rustem.

The stars of tears were shed, cries increased,
The moment of his death has become a sign of judgment day.

Everywhere has filled with cries, sighs, and tears,
Old and young, everyone cried without stopping.

The tears flooded and flew to the lands,
I wonder if the sultan of the world is on the bed of happiness now?

He, the soul of men became earth,
Is it fair that the evil-doer Satan is alive?

Don't put our sighs on the ground like the evening wind,
They insulted the line of our sultans."

Rustem tried very hard to have Yahya executed for the fantastic and shocking elegy, which pointed to Rustem as the murderer of the future sultan. However, Sultan Suleiman prohibited the execution but approved the poet's exile out of Istanbul. Yahya was sent to the Balkans, where he originally came from, but there are disagreements on the exact location where he settled to live. According to some sources, he lived the remainder of his days in the village of *Zvornik*, which is the present-day city in *Bosnia and Herzegovina*.

Undeniably, Yahya did not have any involvement with the death of Mustafa, and additionally, there is clear evidence that he was very much upset at the murder of Mustafa that he wrote the above tragic and upsetting elegy. Due to writing the elegy, Yahya was exiled out of the capital city for the rest of his life. Sadly, there is not much known about Yahya during his exile, after the infamous year of 1553, furthermore, his burial site to this day is unknown.

CHAPTER FIVE

The chosen one for the throne

"To me, the thing that is worse than death is betrayal. You see, I could conceive death, but I could not conceive betrayal." --- Malcolm X

"This black tent of the world was like a two-headed dragon." --- Taslica Yahya (poem written for Mustafa)

"Hear my heart, a heart that screams out for you. If you are going to love me, love me properly" --- Lyrics from the Turkish song titled, Just love me back, a song by Muslum Gurses (writers - Ali Tekinture and Ugur Bayar)

Let us do what is best in novels, try hard to construct sentences and paragraphs, explaining and writing an entertaining, intriguing, and educational telling of a fascinating life lived, without repeating what has already been written about Mustafa, in the prior four chapters. The sentence-layer will bring forward further unknown information about him, in this chapter. This chapter will be the life of Mustafa, up until the infamous day of October 6, 1553, when he dismounted his horse, in front of his sultan father's large black tent. The proceeding act of Mustafa entering the black tent will be written in chapter six.

His life cut extremely short, before many grandeur achievements for both Mustafa and the empire, which could have been commented by historians now, "what if Mustafa was not strangled?"

The course of the empire would have changed since the successive sultans would have been from his descendants, therefore, definitely, the linage of the next sultans would have been different, that is a definite - yes. But let us not go there, where you ask? Many historians and followers of Mustafa, state, "the empire would have survived years and years longer if Mustafa was the next sultan after Suleiman." This comment cannot be confirmed or rejected, since we will never know this. Yes, during Mustafa's reign, the empire would have achieved greatness and prominence not reached during Sultan Selim II's reign (Suleiman's son, Mustafa's half brother, and the next sultan of the empire, after Suleiman), the sentence-layer can sign off on that last sentence. But, an empire that survived longer, past the date of April 23, 1920, which was the end date of the Ottoman Empire, can not be commented on properly, just because Mustafa was the next sultan, after Lawmaker Sultan Suleiman; that will be left to the readers' imagination.

There are unknown and not yet written facts about the well-loved prince. The sentence-layer should get going now, there is still a ton of information to write about.

Prince Mustafa, the protagonist, the **hope** of the people, the **hope** of the empire was born on August 6, 1515, in Manisa, when Suleiman was still just a prince, and the sultan was - Stern Sultan Selim, Mustafa's grandfather.

Mustafa was a Leo. The Leo sign is of a lion, and the name Leo comes from the Latin name for Lion - Leo. As a Leo, he was quick to react, showed power and courage, sincerely an enthusiast, and a brave being. Furthermore, as stated on most horoscope brochures, the characteristics of a person with a Leo sign states the following, "you are friendly and prefer to be clear with everyone from the beginning to avoid any disappointment. You seem to spend a lot of time with your family and are quite happy to help others in key moments. You are very active and seem to take a lot of risks to accomplish your goals. You are very ambitious and stubborn, consequently, hate it when plans don't go the way it was planned. You are devoted and generous to those close." A perfect few sentences describing the prince, interestingly the description was found in a brochure, written in the 21st century, long after the passing of Mustafa.

Why was Mustafa regarded as the **hope** of the people? The sentence-layer should answer this question in one sentence for the time being now, since Mustafa has been referred to many times previously as the **hope** of the people. The reason he was the **hope** of the people was basically that Mustafa was representing the opposite political faction than Sultan Suleiman.

This opposite political faction will be further elaborated in this chapter, but for the time being, a chronological telling of Mustafa's life will continue.

The young prince was the oldest son of Lawmaker Sultan Suleiman and his companion, Mahidevran Gulbahar Sultan. Mustafa lived in the southwest city of Manisa, at the Manisa governing palace with his mother and prince father, for the first five years of his life. Afterward, he accompanied his parents to Istanbul, in the year 1520, when his father was crowned the Ottoman sultan, at the passing of Stern Sultan Selim.

He was liked, respected, and treasured while living at the Topkapi Palace in Istanbul. When he was only nine years old, the Venetian ambassador and traveler named Luigi Bassano reported, "he has extraordinary talent, he will be a warrior; is much loved by the janissaries, and performs great feats."

Mustafa lived at the Topkapi Palace until his 18th birthday and was afterward, sent to govern a territory within the empire, to learn and to acquire the skills required to become a future sultan. He became the governor of the following cities, these were:
Manisa, from 1533 to 1541, (from the age 18 to 26),
Amasya, from 1541 to 1549, (from the age 26 to 34), and
Konya, from 1549 to 1553, (from the age 34 to his death, at age 38).

Describing Mustafa's governor court, the Venetian ambassador,

Luigi Bassano wrote that the prince had, "a most wonderful and glorious court, no less than that of his father," and the Venetian went on to state that, "his mother, who was with him, instructs him in how to make himself loved by the people."

Additionally, Mustafa had other governing duties that were more important and stressful that helped him gain invaluable skills in leadership and governance. When the sultan and high percentage of the large Ottoman army were away on the *Irakein Campaign* (war against Iran - 6th campaign of Suleiman) in the years between 1533 to 1536 and *Corfu Campaign* in the summer of 1537 (war against the combined forces of Venetia and the Pope - 7th campaign of Suleiman), Mustafa stayed behind as he was promoted the *Anatolian Guard General* to protect any attacks from faraway other neighbors against the empire.

Also, when the sultan and the Ottoman army were away on the *Budapest Campaign* (war against the Hungarian Empire - 9th campaign of Suleiman) in the summer of 1541, Mustafa stayed behind as he was promoted to the *Istanbul Guard General* to protect the Topkapi Palace and everyone else in the city from potential attacks from neighbors against the capital city.

Often, when other princes' reached a certain age, late teens, or thereabouts, they stopped focusing on furthering their learning, expanding their networks, and acquiring valuable experience, however, that was not the case for Mustafa, he continued to search and broaden his knowledge in many fields. Especially in the city of Amasya and continued in Konya; Mustafa was involved in furthering his education in Arts, Science, Philosophy, and Religion.

He took intensive lessons from learned scholars within the Ottoman Empire. The few names of the scholars that apprenticed Mustafa are written below, granted, these names are not well known outside of the old Ottoman lands. Therefore, the sentence-layer will write the names of the scholars below, without a lengthy profile for each one of them, researching these wise individuals will be left to the readers; the intellectuals were:

Mustafa Sururi Efendi (*Efendi meaning Lord*) (personal teacher of Mustafa from the time Mustafa came to Istanbul at age five),

Celalzade Salih Celebi (*Celebi meaning Gentleman*) (writer of history, jurisprudence, and literature),

Hayreddin Hızır Efendi (Imam and translator of religious texts), and

Muhyiddin Mehmed Huseyni Efendi (Governor of İstanbul during the early years of Sultan Suleiman's reign).

Similar to his sultan father, Mustafa wrote poetry, under the pen name of *Muhlisi*, the pen name meaning *Sincere* or *Genuine*, and one of his examples is written to show how deep, thoughtful, and interesting his writings were, here below now is a short example:
"If this state thou seeks like the world adorning sun's array,
Lowly it is as if water rubs thy face in earth's dust every day.

Fair to see, but short enduring is this picture bright, the world,
This is a proverb, fleeting like the realm of dreams is earth's display.

Through the needle of its eyelash never hath the heart's thread past,
Like unto the Lord Messiah bide as I half road on the way.

Athlete of the universe through self-reliance grows the heart,
With the ball, the sphere - time fortune - like an apple doth it plays.

Muhlisi, thy frame was formed from but one drop, yet, wonder great!
When thou verses sing, thy spirit like the ocean swells, they say."

Mustafa's pen name was Muhlisi, do the readers remember what the pen name of Sultan Suleiman was? Think back to chapter two. Sultan Suleiman's pen name was Muhibbi, and the similarity of both pen names should be enough to conclude this story now, yes, Prince Mustafa, should have been the next sultan of the empire. That's it, wrap it up folks, we are done.

Wait, wait one second, before closing the book, the sentence-layer requires writing further, we made it thus far, let us continue to that terrible day of the strangulation.

Why was Mustafa regarded as the **hope** of the people and why was there a devoted call for him to be the next ruler of the empire? let us expand on the short answer given earlier. Mustafa was representing the opposite political faction than Sultan Suleiman, that was the reason written above. Furthermore, the janissary army, religious scholars, and the Ottoman general public were supporting the ascension of Mustafa. This was the time of Sultan Suleiman, the Magnificent, however, it was not so a magnificent and wonderful time for the common people in the empire. The constant wars put pressure on the economy that was not doing very well, plus the excessive taxes put heavy pressure on the people, especially on the poorer people in the Balkans, Anatolia, Middle-east, and Northern Africa, basically, every poor or poorer person living inside the empire.

Mustafa held considerable power and a great deal of credibility among various powerful social groups, which were written about already, but one group that held him in high esteem was the janissary army. He earned the support and respect of the janissaries in action and generosity while governing multiple locations in the empire. Venetian ambassador Bernardo Navagero validates this circumstance and stated the following, "one cannot describe how much he is loved and desired by all in the empire to succeed. The janissaries want him, and they let this be known manifestly. There is no Turk or slave of the *Gran-Signor*, who does not have the same opinion or desire because in addition to being the firstborn, which should rightfully give him the throne of the empire, his reputation as courageous, generous, and fair, makes everybody desire for him as the next ruler."

Mustafa was appointed as the Istanbul Guard General, during the Budapest campaign. An example of the janissary love and respect for Mustafa was during this appointment in 1541. Mustafa had to travel from Manisa, his governorship home, to the capital city of Istanbul.

Before arriving at the borders of Istanbul, a large army of janissaries, numbers reported to be around 20,000, stood ready, waiting for him to enter the city. After seeing Mustafa and his men riding towards the capital, the janissaries chanted repeatedly, "Prince Mustafa, our leader our destiny." The chanting did not end but got only louder, finally, the army settled down, when Mustafa stood in-front of them and raised his right arm to thank all of them, for the welcome.

Afterward, the 20,000 janissaries accompanied Mustafa to the Topkapi Palace. When Sultan Suleiman witnessed this love for Mustafa by the janissaries, he almost changed his mind to leave the capital city for the campaign in Budapest, against the Hungarian Empire.

Also, the janissaries, considered Sultan Suleiman old and his choices of the grand viziers were poor since almost none were able to lead proper military campaigns, they wished Mustafa to ascend the throne even before the sultan's death. They wanted to see Sultan Mustafa lead the army in a decisive defeat of the Safavid Empire in the eastern frontier, plus, secure the western borders against the Europeans.

Some historians believe that the start of the weakening of the Ottoman Empire, began with Sultan Suleiman since he over-extended the resources rather thin. The sentence-layer partially agrees with this point of view, however, believes that the slow weakening did not start during Suleiman's rule, but right after him, during the reign of his son, Sultan Selim II. Troubled times were just around the corner, as Suleiman's latter year policies were not necessarily proper for the empire, and this showed and blossomed during the next regime of the empire.

Mustafa was looked upon by everyone to slow the empire's constant wars, improve the economy by improving on Suleiman's tactics with youthful enthusiasm. Plus, the exceptional education received by Mustafa was ready to be applied to the problems growing during these times. Therefore, the political opposition against Suleiman centered around Mustafa, and the prince did not (or could not) stop the janissaries, religious leaders, and the common people's support for his ascension.

Suleiman's father, Stern Sultan Selim overthrew his father (Suleiman's grandfather, Saint Sultan Beyazit II was overthrown from the throne by Stern Sultan Selim) with the help of the janissaries. Consequently, Suleiman was paranoid, and constantly thought about the answer to the following question, *"Is Mustafa going to overthrow me, this year?"* This question was constantly on his mind; the coming revolt against him by Mustafa was inevitable, he thought. Furthermore, Mustafa's outward appearance and actions resembled his father's, and this gave Suleiman further worry, as looking at him, he remembered his father, Stern Sultan Selim.

Also, there was Hurrem, who desired to eliminate Mustafa, as she wanted to secure the throne for one of her sons. Hurrem acted to save the lives of her sons, given that Mustafa was considered the favorite to become the next sultan. Therefore, hearing and seeing Suleiman act in a paranoid manner, increased Hurrem's anxiety, and she knew that the time was approaching rapidly for her to act accordingly to save her son's and secure the Ottoman throne.

Every prince in the empire had the right to ascend to the throne since the empire could not be dividable, therefore, competition between surviving princes led to fratricide. The law of fratricide was codified in Ottoman Law and set forth by Conqueror Sultan Mehmet II, the great great grandfather of Mustafa (Mustafa's father was Lawmaker Sultan Suleiman, Suleiman's father was Stern Sultan Selim, Selim's father was Saint Sultan Beyazit II, and Beyazit's father was Conqueror Sultan Mehmet II).

The law of fratricide states, "for the welfare of the state, one of my sons to whom God grants the sultanate may lawfully put his brothers to death. A majority of the religious scholars consider this act permissible." With this code in place by Conqueror Sultan Mehmet II, fratricide was acceptable and customary. The law, not only justified the practice of fratricide but also established that a would-be sultan needed to act as written in the law.

However, there was evidence from the actions and character of Mustafa that this bloody and outdated practice of fratricide was not going to be utilized if Mustafa made it to the throne. Mustafa had respectful, civil, and loving relationships with all of his younger step-brothers, particularly with Prince Cihangir. He was not going to pursue the path of killing his brothers, he was in favor of giving his younger brothers a territory to rule within the empire, while he was the sultan.

After Suleiman completed his ventures, as in, expanded the empire in prior years, he began to favor the less aggressive and warlike foreign policy, during the early 1540s. Suleiman preferred to stay at Topkapi Palace, instead of going on the road to conquer neighboring lands, plus, he increasingly retracted from politics and withdrew into self-relaxation and rest.

Also, Suleiman was witnessing the growing tension between his wives, Hurrem and Mahidevran, both were plotting and planning for their sons to secure the throne. Suleiman was growing fearful that eventually, the tension would spill over to his sons, and he would witness the bloody battle between them during his lifetime. This was another reason why, he did not want to leave Topkapi Palace, as he did not want one of his sons to displace him from the throne. Furthermore, he was well aware of Mustafa's reputation and prominence, by every social group in the empire, and he was recognizing that Mustafa could be the one to unseat him from the throne.

The social groups within the empire noticed with despair that Suleiman was absent from being the military commander, and he had left the management and ruling of the empire to his Grand Vizier and son-in-law Rustem Pasha. This especially upset the janissaries, who preferred a sultan that was more active with the affairs of the empire.

Toward the late 1540s and into the early 1550s, the silent rivalry between Mustafa and the sons of Hurrem to secure the throne became more apparent and public. The *Habsburg Empire* ambassador to Istanbul, *Gerhard Veltwyck* wrote a letter to his emperor, in the letter, there was following written, "Grand Vizier Rustem Pasha wants to eliminate Prince Mustafa to secure the throne for Selim. Hurrem Sultan, her daughter Mihrimah, and Rustem are all collaborating to assist the ascension of either Selim or Beyazit to the throne."

Grand Vizier Rustem Pasha married Mihrimah Sultan, who was the only daughter of Suleiman and Hurrem. The marriage made him part of the sultanate family, which was headed by his mother-in-law, Hurrem. Like his mother-in-law, Rustem desired that Suleiman be succeeded by one of Hurrem's sons, Selim or Beyazit. Rustem wanted one of Hurrem's sons to sit on the throne, this would allow him to maintain his power as the grand vizier and control the government. Hence, Mustafa's death would be very beneficial and serve Rustem's interests.

It is on record that Rustem tried to damage Mustafa's reputation, in the eyes of Suleiman. Two examples can be written, the first example is in 1549, when bandits from the neighboring northeastern country of Georgia killed the governor of Erzurum. Mustafa, from his close-proximity governorship post in Amasya, requested help from Istanbul to attack the Georgian bandits. However, Rustem refused to send assistance to Mustafa, analyzing smartly that the prince would gain even more prestige in the eyes of everyone when he defeated the Georgians.

The second example was in the following year of 1550. A gang of thieves from another neighboring country, this time Persia, crossed the eastern border into Ottoman lands and robbed several small villages in Anatolia. Mustafa again appealed for help from Istanbul, but Rustem refused to send assistance again.

Rustem grudgingly recognized and fully knew that if the people heard further accomplishments of Mustafa, there would be more prestige and honor given to him, from all social groups in the empire. Not him, the grand vizier, or the sultan could stop the further raised voices by everyone wanting, no not wanting, demanding Mustafa crowned the next sultan immediately.

Before leaving Istanbul, Suleiman sent a messenger to Mustafa asking his son to join him in Eregli. Mustafa discussed his sultan father's demand for a meeting him with his three advisors, who collectively advised him not to go to his father's camp. The advisors insisted that if he were to go to the meeting, he would perhaps lose his life. Understandably, the decision was very difficult, and it was not an easy decision to make for Mustafa, he thought, "should I stay, or should I go?"

The Habsburg Empire's ambassador Monsieur Ogier Ghiselin de Busbecq, who had visited Mustafa, informed his emperor of the dilemma Mustafa was facing, Busbecq wrote, "Mustafa hesitated between two choices, if he entered the presence of his father and found him angry and offended, he would certainly be at risk. But if he avoided him, he would be known publicly that he contemplated an act of treason. The decision he took is the one that required more courage and risk. Leaving the seat of his government, he headed to his father's camp, which lay not far off, relying on his innocence; he was probably also confident that no harm could come to him in the presence of the army. Be that as it may, he went to meet an inevitable death".

Mustafa finally decided to obey his father and join the sultan's army, reportedly telling his three advisors that he could not resist going, he had said, "where destiny casts me, there is where I will go."

The legitimacy of a sultan was to some extent based on his effect-iveness as a warrior on the battlefield, that is, in leading the army to victory. When a sultan died, the right to rule preferably passed to the prince who was most courageous and most capable of lead-ing the army to further success. The competition between the princes', during the time that his sultan father was still alive, was in a sense an arena in which each prince had the chance to demon-strate their competence and capacity to become a warrior sultan.

Prince Mustafa appeared more courageous and spirited when compared to his younger brothers. Due to his leadership and mili-tary prowess, Mustafa attracted extensive support from diverse segments within the Ottoman society, during a time when his sultan father, seemed content to settle down in Istanbul and less eager to act out on the warrior characteristics required for a sul-tan.

Mustafa, for his part, did not ignore the enthusiasm of the people. He wanted his right to the throne respected and worked to gather important people around him. An example of this was when he disclosed his ambition and desire in a letter to the governor *Ayas Pasha* of the faraway eastern city of *Erzurum*. Mustafa expressed openly his desire for the throne, although he clearly stated that he would not overthrow his father and wished to be sultan only after his sultan father died.

Also, Mustafa had been in communication with the Republic of Venetia, nobleman, and ambassador Domenico Trevisano. The Venetian ambassador dispatched a letter to the Venetian Council and Senate on September 15, 1553, indicating that Mustafa sent a messenger named, *Nebi Bey*, to him, asking help from Venice to se-cure the Ottoman throne.

Afterward, Nebi Bey traveled to Venice with precious gifts to ne-gotiate with the Venetian council and senate for the support and backing of Mustafa to the Ottoman throne. The Venetians were willing to support Mustafa if he agreed to return the former Venetian stronghold lands in *Morea* (present-day southern Greece).

When Nebi Bey was sent out for Istanbul, he was carrying a letter from Venice, to Mustafa. However, Mustafa never lived to see his messenger return, as he was executed the same day Nebi Bey sailed out from Venice, which was October 6, 1553.

The Venetian ambassador in Istanbul sent a letter on October 15, 1553, to the Venetian Council and Senate advising them that Mustafa was strangled by Sultan Suleiman. The news of Mustafa's death was a complete shock to the Venetians.

This futile episode of diplomacy, between Mustafa and the Venetian Council and Senate, showed that during the early 1550s there were working relationships to secure the Ottoman throne. Similar to Hurrem Sultan and her son-in-law Grand Vizier Rustem Pasha working diligently and discreetly to secure the throne for one of her sons, Prince Mustafa was also trying to bolster relationships to lock the throne for himself.

Forming alliances and seeking supporters by both Mustafa and Hurrem, were reasonable actions to secure the throne, this is acceptable in everyone's opinion. Additionally, supporting a particular candidate constituted a way for various groups within or outside the empire, these being, faraway neighbors, viziers, janissaries, scholars, and the citizens to participate in the imperial politics.

Forming alliances and seeking support is perfectly acceptable, however, accusing someone of betrayal is not acceptable. That was the difference between Hurrem Sultan and her accomplices' action when compared to Mustafa's. Hurrem Sultan and her accomplices accused Mustafa falsely of rebellion and betrayal against his sultan father. They knew that the word betrayal had a heavy consequence in the Ottoman Empire. Any person that was found to have betrayed the sultan, the throne, or the empire was killed instantly. Consequently, they knew if the Lawmaker Sultan Suleiman heard that his eldest son betrayed him, that would be the end of him, the end of Mustafa.

Sadly, the death of Mustafa came soon after the false betrayal accusations began.

CHAPTER SIX

The big shock that upset the people

"Justice will not be served until those who are unaffected are as outraged as those who are." --- Benjamin Franklin

"Sultan of the world was standing with anger, like fire." --- Taslica Yahya (poem written for Mustafa)

"All I want is peace and love on this planet. Ain't that how God planned it?" --- Lyrics from the rap song, Fear of a black planet, by the group, Public Enemy (writer - Chuck D)

Up until this point in the story, everything written is accurate and a fact. Granted, it is a strong statement, which could be retorted by a reader, with one line that could show something other than what was written in this story. However, the sentence-layer is confident of the truth of the story told up until this point, and welcomes any critique.

Nevertheless, most, if not all readers will not object to anything written thus far. Therefore, it would be acceptable to write that, thus far, this is a non-fiction story of the Ottoman Empire, up until the current time, current time meaning - Lawmaker Sultan Suleiman's time.

However, most everything in this current chapter will be a fictional telling of what happened when Prince Mustafa rode into the campsite and entered the big black tent, where his sultan father was waiting for him. The phrase most everything will be fiction means that there still are parts in this chapter that will be accurate. Therefore, the readers will truly have an entertaining, interesting, and surprising chapter ahead of them.

Many sources give detailed information of when Mustafa entered the black tent, but no information is available of what happened inside, other than Mustafa being strangled in there. What do we know of that dreadful day? We know the following:
Mustafa arrived at the Ottoman camp,
Mustafa met his sultan father inside the black tent,
Mustafa was inside the tent for less than one hour,
Mustafa did not have blood stains anywhere on his body,
Mustafa was strangled, and
Mustafa never came out alive.

Nevertheless, as written above, no information is available of what happened inside, other than Mustafa being strangled in the black tent. The sentence-layer will now do his very best, the craftiest possible way to try and relay to the esteemed readers what happened in the tent. The story will be told still in third-person narration, which means, it will be the sentence-layers telling of Mustafa's story.

Now let us start the fictional telling, from the fall season, of the infamous year of 1553.

In the late summer of the year 1553, precisely on August 28, Lawmaker Sultan Suleiman left Istanbul with a 50,000 strong Ottoman army for his campaign in the east, against the Safavid Empire. Before his departure, he dispatched a letter to his eldest son Mustafa, the **hope** of the people was ordered to join this campaign against the eastern Safavids. Suleiman, along with his army arrived at the town of Eregli on October 5, one day before the meeting with his eldest son.

Despite the warnings from within his support group, particularly his mother, Mahidevran, Mustafa decided to still join his sultan father's army at Eregli, which was just on the outskirts of the good-sized city of Konya.

Mustafa told his small group of advisors that he could not refrain from going to meet his sultan father. It would have been not easy, almost impossible for him to disobey his father's orders, given that his sultan father was openly accusing him of rebellion and betrayal against the throne and the mighty empire.

The ambassador Monsieur Ogier Ghiselin de Busbecq, wrote the following about the heavy decision that faced the young prince, "Mustafa hesitated between two choices, if he entered the presence of his father and found him angry and offended, he would certainly be at risk. But if he avoided him, he would be known publicly that he contemplated an act of treason. The decision he took is the one that required more courage and risk. Leaving the seat of his government, he headed to his father's camp, which lay not far off, relying on his innocence; he was probably also confident that no harm could come to him in the presence of the army. Be that as it may, he went to meet an inevitable death".

Mustafa obeyed his father and made plans to join the sultan's army, reportedly telling his three advisors that he did not want to resist going, he had said, "where destiny casts me, there is where I will go."

On the morning of October 6, Mustafa, who was then the governor of Konya, left his governorship home, very early in the morning. He meet his protection of six elite janissary soldiers and they prepared for the horseback ride to the neighboring town, where Suleiman's army was camped.

As the young prince came close to the camp, the chanting began from the large army of janissaries, they recognized the future leader of the empire, and could not resist, and started the repeated chants of, "Prince Mustafa, our leader our destiny. Prince Mustafa, our leader our destiny. Prince Mustafa, our leader our destiny." The chanting only ended, when Mustafa came to his final destination, in front of the big black tent, which would mean that it was a full ten minutes of loud chanting in the camp. The few dozen opponents of the young prince, the ten minutes felt like an eternity, as the chanting hurt their sensitive and delicate ears. But, for the ones that loved him, which was ninety nine percent of the janissaries, it was delirium, and an absolute joy to see their leader arrive on a brown-colored horse.

The Lawmaker was inside the large black tent, of that dreadful and infamous day. He was sitting on a comfortable baldachin throne seat, made of rich walnut wood, waiting impatiently, for his eldest son to enter into it. He heard the loud chants, "Prince Mustafa, our leader our destiny. Prince Mustafa, our leader our destiny. Prince Mustafa, our leader our destiny," and put his arms-up quickly, and covered his sagging hairy ears with his boney blue vein mapped hands.

Mustafa and his men dismounted from their individual horses in-front of the sultan's black tent. He was here now, in front of the tent, to show respect and to show that he was obeying his father. He wanted all the naysayers, as surely there were men in the Lawmaker's circle that spoke among themselves, "Mustafa will not show, he betrayed Sultan Suleiman, he will not have the courage to come to meet his father." The naysayers were completely stunned and amazed that Mustafa showed his face, furthermore, they were silently impressed by his loyalty to his sultan father.

The young prince came to the camp because he also wanted the opportunity to talk with his father in private, he wanted a father and son meeting. The meeting would be to tell him that the accusations were all false, there was no betrayal activity against the throne, furthermore, there would never be one in the future.

The Lawmaker was still seated on the comfortable throne seat, waited a few seconds extra after the chanting had subdued. He wanted to be sure, waited, heard nothing outside the tent, the chanting had stopped. Thankfully, it was quiet and peaceful again, the way he liked it. He dropped his arms onto his thighs, the hands hitting the thighs made a noise, similar to two branches hitting each other, when a strong wind storm was in effect.

Mustafa and his protection of six elite janissary soldiers were standing at the front of the tent, the soldier's duties were extremely difficult, these were:
Keep the prince away from trouble,
Keep the prince safe, and (most importantly),
Keep the prince alive.

The Lawmaker was inside the large black colored tent, waiting, thinking, and still weighing all the information given to him, by the Grand Vizier, Rustem Pasha. What information was given to the sultan? There were lengthy letters written to neighboring empires for dethroning the Lawmaker. All the letters contained the signature of his eldest son, albeit the signatures were fake, however, Suleiman did not know this very important and critical part. The Lawmaker had deep dark lines prevalent on his forehead, mostly caused by the constant anxiety and unease he had over the decision made. Three nights before at Topkapi Palace, prior to leaving for the eastern campaign; he made the shocking decision to have his eldest son killed by strangulation.

This statement of, he made the shocking decision, was not fully accurate, what happened was that Lawmaker sent a lengthy letter to Seyhulislam Ebussuud Efendi (*Seyhulislam* means the *Religious leader of the Ottoman Empire*), explaining his version of the story to the religious leader. Lawmaker's version stated that Mustafa had betrayed the empire. After explaining to the religious leader the situation, Lawmaker asked the vital question, *is it proper and permissible to execute my son?*

The religious leader, Ebussuud Efendi received the letter from Sultan Suleiman and answered back, by writing back to the Lawmaker. The letter was detailed, plus it contained numerous passages from the Quran, supporting his conclusion. After writing about the passages from the Quran and giving detailed explanations, the religious leader, put the following parable, comparing

Lawmaker's current situation to another individuals:

"It is said that God gives the right amount of snow to the mountain. You, being the sultan of an empire that controls seven different time zones, and similar to a great mountain, is standing straight up and strong.

As you will have a spring and summer time in your life, there will also be the fall and winter seasons.

I found a solution to your problem. I believe this solution that I found, will send you to the daylight from a long black night you have been in. God-willing, you will be delivered from darkness to bright sunshine in your soul.

I will tell you a brief story now and the answer you are seeking is there.

Once upon a time, there was a business-man who was doing very well, abundant gold coins followed into his abode. The business-man was required to go on a lengthy trip, granted in those days, going away, meant that you would be on the road for months at a time. He left his family and business in the care of his son, the son he loved the most. He had complete trust and belief in his son. However, this son instead of taking care of the family and business, he tried to kill all of the family members, take possession of the business and assets, and went even further, he tried to have his father killed. Now, I ask you, what would a reasonable person do to a son such as the one described above?

Answer: If a son by force, tries to take possession of his father's assets, he plans deceit against his father, he harms and tortures, his own family, then it is acceptable and comprehensible to kill this evil tyrant."

The answer in his bony blue vein mapped hands, as in the letter in his hands, with the answer that it was acceptable to kill his son, the Lawmaker made plans at Topkapi Palace to have his son meet him at the town of Eregli.

The Lawmaker sitting inside the black tent, on October 6, was confident that executing his son was justifiable, and the religious leader of the Ottoman Empire had permitted him to do this. Nonetheless, he was still anxious, and the deep dark lines in his forehead proved this. He was still wrestling with the idea in his mind, and repeatedly asked the question to himself, "should I give the order to execute my son?"

When did the Lawmaker decide to execute his son? The answer is unknown, as it was guessed that the Lawmaker made the final decision that day. Furthermore, sources provide no hint as to the time of the final decision made by the Lawmaker. Ambassador Monsieur Ogier Ghiselin de Busbecq, confirms that the Lawmaker received the legal letter from Ebussuud Efendi, but cannot give further information to a precise time when the decision was made to execute Mustafa.

Mustafa stood by his brown horse, in front of the black as death colored tent, looking, examining the current situation, he right there and then realized that there were a lot more of his sultan father's janissary men, standing all around the black tent, this was not common, he whispered in his mind, his voice surprised him as it was barely audible and hoarse, *"why are there three dozen janissaries here, waiting for me, when usually there were at most, only the four soldiers at the entrance."* He answered himself, *"my wise sultan father knows best."*

His mother's written warning letter flashed in his mind. Mustafa had read the letter three times, back to back, when he first received it last night and remembered the entirety of it. The letter stated: "My love, my wealth, my one and only son Mustafa. You are my very existence and joy, I pray to the almighty that you receive this letter, and I pray to him again that you are alive, in good condition, and good health.

I have bad news to relay to you today, and I am confident that you will take my heed to heart, and listen to your mother, who values you, who loves you, like nothing else on this shameful world - a shameful world, where a father plots to kill his son.

Yes, you read that correctly. Please listen to your mother, my heart is aching in fear and worry at this moment. Please turn around immediately and ride back to your home, to your family, to your governorship home.

I have received word from a reliable vizier at Topkapi Palace that on your meeting with your sultan father at Eregli, there will be a plot to kill you. I believe this to be a sincere and true warning, as your sultan father has not put together common sense to create a logical thought, since Hurrem entered his life, therefore, please listen to your mother, and DO NOT GO TO MEET YOUR FATHER.

I cannot bear to hear or see any harm come to you, just the thought of it has my hands and knees shaking. I am very much distressed currently, waiting impatiently to see you again. Please, return home to us my springtime, my summer, my only happiness.
May the almighty help all of us, but help you the most.

Your loving mother – Mahidevran."

He realized that he should have listened to his dear mother, and stayed away from this camp. The young prince whispered in his mind again, his voice still barely audible, *"how could I deny my sultan father's request to stay away?"* He answered himself, *"I had to come and meet him, or I would have been called a deceiver, I could not live to hear that. I had to come."*

Mustafa turned to look at his six elite protection of janissaries, they all gave each other a look that screamed, without moving their mouths, *"keep calm, let us try to get through this ordeal."*

The chanting had completely stopped, and the Lawmaker sat on his throne listening for any activity outside of the big black tent. He strained his neck forward, held it there for five seconds, to hear if there was a conversation outside; there was none of that. He was still seated on his walnut wood throne, waiting. Around the sultan, in the deep dark corners of the black shadowy tent, there were men in wait, men whose duty were to obey the sultan's every command. What was that common phrase used? "You say jump; I say how high." In this case, when the sultan clapped his boney blue vein mapped hands, the men in the deep dark corners would jump into action, similar to a thoroughbred racehorse that jumps out when released from the starting gate.

The **hope** of the people inhaled a deep breath and let it out, left his horse behind, and walked towards the entrance to meet the high-ranking state officers, who were standing at the entrance, while the three dozen janissary soldiers were all around, ready to go off like a pistol that was cocked. The prince's six elite protection stood behind, their big hands tightly wrapped around the muzzle of their swords, watching, as their leader walked towards the entrance of the black tent. The entrance was wide open, but dark, nothing could be seen inside the tent. The entrance resembled the mouth of a hungry wild dragon; open mount, but nothing else visible, but black darkness.

The Lawmaker made as if to stand up, but instead, he re-positioned himself while seated. He put his boney blue vein mapped hands on his upper thighs, pushed his chest forward, and straightened his back, he resembled an old rooster that had seen better days, a rooster with a thin torso, under the faded few feathers. He was preparing himself to see his eldest son and to show him who was still the sultan of this mighty empire.

Mustafa was wearing all-whites today, except for his boots and sash, which were black colored, the items worn by him were as follows:
Black shiny boots that went up to his lower calves,
White clean trousers that were baggy around the upper legs,
White long-sleeved dress shirt with buttons that did not have a collar,
Black thick sash around his waist, which contained two small

curved knives,
White vest,
White long kaftan with fur lining and embroidery that went all the way down to his upper boots,
A heavy metal sword hanging on his left hip, held there by a black leather belt, which was wrapped around his waist, and
White small turban on his head.

Mustafa truly looked like a prince who was well taken care of by his staff at the governorship home. Furthermore, wearing white was a smart choice today, since the color white meant what? When referring to *Merriam Webster dictionary*, the word white has a lengthy explanation, but basically, this color means:
Free from spot or blemish,
Symbol of purity,
Clean and fresh, and
Innocent.

Whether the young prince wore white purposefully on that day or it was a simple coincidence is unknown. However, his outfit did reflect his innocence, if one had the intelligence to observe this, and put it together. In other words, it was obvious as the nose on one's face, that Mustafa was wearing white and this reflected his innocence and purity.

The eldest son of Suleiman stood in front of the entrance to the tent, he was told nervously by one of the high ranking state officers, "my prince, I need you to give me, all of your equipment now, all of them," this meant that he needed to hand over his sword and knives, before entering the tent to meet the sultan. Mustafa glared at the high-ranking officer, but the officer could not hold the gaze of the prince, and timidly turned his eyes and head away. This request was never before made to him, he was always allowed to keep his equipment when accompanying his sultan father, nonetheless, he did not object, he could not. He unhooked his one heavy metal sword passed it over, afterwards, he gave his two small knives to the state officer.

Mustafa was now without protection. This was not good.

The Lawmaker sat on his walnut wood throne, waiting, his hands resting on his bony upper thighs. The long skinny crooked fingers extended out from the oversized crimson cloak sleeves. His fingernails were perfectly manicured but dull and dark yellow-colored, the color was like yucky mucus blown out into a handkerchief, if one cared to peak after the blow.

Before entering the dark and shadowy large tent, Mustafa glanced back again at his six elite protection of janissary soldiers that were standing meters away, and he made a slow-motion with his head, a motion of nodding up and down, to mean, *"just stay cool, it will be alright."* Plus, there was a nervous crooked smile on his face, overall he was trying very hard to send the message to his elite protection of janissaries, the message of, *"stay calm,"* and, *"wait for me to exit the tent."*

The young prince failed miserably to keep his elite janissary protection of men from staying calm, they were very worried, similar to six men in a small yellow rubber boat, stuck on a pond at *Everglades National Park in Florida*, with three dozen crocodiles swimming around them. The men were right to be worried, the odds were not in their favor but they stayed put, and waited tensely with their big hands wrapped around the muzzle of their swords. The janissary men watched as their leader, their **hope** entered the mouth of the wild boar, this was the last time, they would see him alive.

The elite janissary men had failed to keep their leader alive. What were the objectives of the men? The objectives were:
Keep the prince away from trouble,
Keep the prince safe, and (most importantly),
Keep the prince alive.

The most important duty for the men was to keep Mustafa alive, but they failed miserably. Deep down, the men knew that their leader would not come back out alive, but there was a small chance, they thought collectively, *"there is a chance, he will come out alive, right?"* Mustafa had the same chance of walking out of the tent alive, as a person that falls into a cage full of tigers, in a zoo of any large city.

Mustafa walked a few steps slowly into the tent, right after he walked in, the entrance of the tent was snapped shut behind him, he turned back to look, saw nothing but darkness, then turned around to face the center again. It was very much dark inside, the candles were not lit, usually many candles were lit all around, inside the tent, making a welcoming ambiance inside. Today, there was none of that, it was dark as a tomb inside. Consequently, there were dark corners all around him that he could not make out. Plus, his eyes needed time to adjust from the bright day outside to the dark as night tent.

The contrast between the dark black tent and Mustafa's white outfit was rather interesting. The best possible way to describe this contrast would be to ask the esteemed readers, "have you ever seen a white ghost in your dark bedroom, as you were trying to fall asleep?" If the answer is yes, then that is what the young prince looked like, he looked like a floating white object, with nothing but darkness all around him. Surely, the sentence-layer should not have to point this out, nonetheless will anyways, Mustafa looked like a friendly ghost, none of those evil bloody ones.

The young prince took a few slow careful steps forward, stopped, looked, nothing but darkness all around him, enveloping him, similar to a sticky black Anaconda wrapping and squeezing its prey. He looked straight ahead, his eyes were slowly adjusting to the darkness around him, he could now see, be it, barely, he saw someone seated, far in the tent. His father was ten meters away, seated on his wood throne, right in the middle of the tent.

Mustafa whispered a question in his mind, his voice still hoarse, *"was that my father?"* His eyes were better adjusted now, and he realized that it was his father, yes it was him seated, he could see the shiny large high gold crown on his head, long silver-grey beard on his lower face, collar of the crimson-colored cloak was up to his sagging ears, and his dark eyes, very deep in their socket, staring back blankly, *"yes, that was my sultan father, may God help me,"* he whispered inside his mind again.

Since Mustafa knew now that his sultan father was seated, he took quick steps towards him, he was preparing to kneel in front of his father, to kiss his hand, and bring his father's hand towards his own forehead. This gesture of kissing an elder person's hand is a very old custom in these parts, it shows a gesture that indicates courtesy, politeness, respect, and admiration by the younger person toward the elder. After kissing the elder person's hand, the younger one pulls the hand to his own forehead, this is the gesture showing total devotion.

Mustafa was preparing himself for the *hand - kiss - forehead* action but saw the right arm of the Lawmaker go up, with the palm facing the younger man, and the long skinny crooked four fingers pointed up were visible, this action said STOP, the young prince stopped, like a buck caught staring at the headlights of the fast-approaching eighteen-wheeler, he stopped cold. Lawmaker Sultan Suleiman put his arm down, uttered the following sentence assertively, in a cold as ice voice, "you, betrayed me, Mustafam." The m letter added to the name Mustafa, made the word *Mustafam*, which meant *My Mustafa*, *"you betrayed me my Mustafa."*

"I did not betray you...", the reply that automatically came out of the young prince's mouth, but the arm went up again to mean STOP. Mustafa was going to say, "I did not betray you, my sultan," but the sentence was cut short by the right arm. He sensed a heaviness in the air, the young man was nervous and tense, when entering the tent, but just now, seeing the cold manners of his sultan father made him stress and worry. He was extremely worried right about now.

Lawmaker Sultan Suleiman got up slowly from his walnut wood throne, stood, and stared at his son, he looked like that famous vampire from Transylvania. His high crown, looked like a top hat, the vampire liked to wear on occasion. His crimson cloak looked like the long black coat the vampire wore. His long skinny crooked fingers visible by his side, looked like the claws of that famous vampire. And, his sunken deep dark eyes, looked like the vampires, a vampire that had not seen sunlight for 500 years. He said assertively again, in the same cold as ice voice, "may God help you, you are on your own now."

This cold statement made by the Lawmaker requires elaborating. The first part, *"may God help you,"* meant the following:
May God help you, because I will not. I will not help you, since you betrayed me. And what God will help and show sympathy and compassion to a man that betrays his father? I ask you that, what God would? If there is a God that will show sympathy to a son that betrayed his own father, that is the God that can try to help you now. As that God that shows sympathy to a son that betrays his father is no God of mine.

Furthermore, the latter part of the spoken words of the sultan, *"you are on your own now,"* meant as follows:
You are on your own now, and I will show everyone who is in command of this mighty empire. I am going to send the wrath and anger I hold for you, from all corners of my abode, they will beat you down and avenge my good name. My fury will show to you, and your supporters, and our far away neighbors that whoever plans a blow against me, the shadow of the true God on earth, will be shown no mercy. Even my son will be sacrificed to show to everyone, I am Sultan Suleiman, I am the Ottoman Empire. No mercy to any person that betrays me.

The Lawmaker brought both of his boney blue vein mapped hands quickly together in a swift motion and clapped. This quick motion by the sultan and the loud sound of the clap surprised the younger man. The quick motion was unexpected by an old man such as his sultan father, this action amazed him. Moreover, the sound of the thunderous clap, which echoed like a monster's roar inside the tent, scared him. After the loud clap, the Lawmaker put his hands by his sides again, and slowly took a few steps back, away from his eldest son, into the darkness of the back area of the make-shift black tent.

Mustafa was feeling overwhelmed with stress, his blood pressure was rising, and his heart rate increased from the mid 70 beats per minute, when he first entered the tent, to 110 just now, after the thunderous clap. He watched his sultan father take a few steps away from him, and just like that, his father disappeared from his vision. The young prince realized that the big black tent was much bigger and there was another section further ahead of him. He yelled out, "I did not betray you my sultan father!", he waited for a reply back, however, there was none. He yelled out again, "please hear me, I did not betray you! please know this," again, there was no reply back from the Lawmaker.

He took a step forward, toward the direction of his sultan father, but stopped, and listened. Mustafa heard silent footsteps approach him from all corners of the big black tent, this startled him. The corners of the dark black tent, which he thought previously were dark emptiness, were now moving towards him. Yes, the dark emptiness was moving towards him, he could make this out. The black darkness was moving towards him, slowly and silently, like a gray wolf approaching its innocent prey. He was stunned at this revelation.

Mustafa's heart rate increased even more now, his heart was pounding out 125 beats per minute, comparable to a race car at the start line, pulsing, beating, and shaking, trying to ready himself for some unknown torment.

He turned 360 degrees slowly around to look at every corner, which he could now finally make out inside the tent, he counted and saw that there were seven black gear wearing sultan's janissary soldiers. Mustafa quickly reached for his black sash, this was where his sword should have been, however, it was not there. He remembered that his metal sword and small knives were taken from him, before entering the tent, disappointedly, he inhaled and exhaled loudly, and whispered to himself, *"just me, myself, and I, no weapon, against the coming seven, who are showing aggression, to send me to heaven."* He smiled nervously, at his witty rhyme, and realized that his father had clapped his hands and the janissaries came into motion. Recognizing this now, made him angry and sad, both emotions he was experiencing at the same time. He was feeling overwhelmed, *"why were the janissaries closing in on him?"* He whispered in his mind, more seriously this time, but knew the answer.

The black-wearing janissaries were the dark shadows that were hiding in wait, in all corners of the black as death large make-shift tent. The seven shadows were now moving towards him, slowly, one step at a time. The seven janissaries were covered in black: black boots, black pants, black shirt top, and a black mask that covered their faces and head, the only visible features were their big shinny eyes and their stretched out hands, wanting to grab him, wrestle him down, and strangle him. He knew that they would strangle him as it was an Ottoman custom to not spill blood when disposing of a person that was connected by blood to the sultan.

He turned around to complete another full circle and knew that the seven black gear-wearing sultan's janissary soldier's intentions were not good, as explained above. The men were not there to grab him, throw him outside of the tent, and set him free; no that was not the plan. Mustafa knew that these men were here to harm him, they were here, sent by his sultan father to kill him. It was his father who demanded that he meet him inside the tent, it was his father who planned a trap for him, and it was his dear sultan father that wanted him dead. Realizing the fact that his own father planned to kill him, made him have a vision.

He saw himself in a coffin, he laid in the coffin, face-up, but he was still alive. The lid of the coffin was closed, and it was dark inside. Someone from the outside of the coffin was hammering a nail to the lid, to keep the lid from ever coming open again. He extended his arms up in a quick panic-filled motion, trying to force open the lid of the coffin, but he was unsuccessful. He tried to turn over, but could not. It was very claustrophobic inside the coffin, and he was in complete terror, and screamed out, *"I did not betray you."*

The young prince blinked multiple times and now he was having a second vision, he was out of the coffin, and saw himself as a six-year-old child, sitting on his father's lap. Mustafa had beautiful big brown eyes, and the eyes were looking desperately into his father's eyes. He started to speak, *"my sultan father,"* he stopped talking as he was surprised and shocked to hear that his voice did not sound like it belonged to a little six-year-old body. The voice that came out of the six-year-old body was his current voice, a voice of a man who was thirty-eight years old. Mustafa continued nonetheless, *"you, my sultan father, please hear me now, I did not betray you. I need to tell you this now, as I will not get the opportunity to tell you this at a later date. Know that I am innocent, know that you have killed your innocent son. I am dead."*

The **hope** of the people shook his head and came back to the present situation, he spoke out loud, "I am dead, is that what I said?" Yes, that was what he had said, he wanted to change this vision desperately. He was getting ready to defend himself from the seven janissaries that were fulfilling an order, the order was from his sultan father, he could imagine his father saying to the janissary men, *kill him, but be careful, do not spill his blood."* He thought, *"thank you father, for giving the order to kill me, without wanting to spill my blood. It was not all bad after all."*

He was trying to clear his head from the visions, and he needed to focus on the now, the present, the question he had was, *"how will I get out of this mess?"* It was going to be difficult, he knew this, but he was going to try his best to fight them off.

"What about his men?" he thought, were they, meaning the sultan's janissary men, going to kill his elite protection of men? The answer was yes, if he died now, here, his men would be slashed, right outside the tent. He thought, *"I need to stay alive, not only for me but for my men."*

His mind wandered again, he could not help it, he thought about his mother Mahidevran, he thought about his wife *Mihrunnisa*, he thought about his children of *Princess Nergissah, Prince Mehmet*, and *Princess Sah*. What would happen to his immediate family, if the seven janissary men were successful in strangling him? His family would be at the mercy of the Lawmaker, and one of the following would be the outcome to all of them:
Kill them all,
Separate all of them by sending each to different corner of the empire, or
Kill only Prince Mehmet, marry off both princesses, leave the mother and wife alone, for their silent suffering.

All of the above options are incredibly cruel, but the respected readers should know that option number three was going to be the outcome.

Mustafa did not want any harm to come unto his family, *"I need to get out of this tent alive,"* he whispered in his mind.

One of the men in black that was closing in on the young prince had a shiny silver bracelet around his arm, this shiny bracelet flashed in Mustafa's eye, as the janissary was jerking his arm forward toward him. This motion and the flash from the bracelet helped him to zone out from his thoughts, and come back to the current deadly situation.

Mustafa was in a serious predicament, there were seven janissary men around him, closing in on him, similar to a scene from the film titled, Star Wars. In a scene from this film, Princess Lea, Luke Skywalker, Hans Solo, and Chewbacca were caught inside a garbage bin, and the walls were closing in on them, to crush both the garbage and them. This scene from the film was comparable to the current situation facing the young prince, the men were closing in on him now.

None of the janissary men had swords or knives in their hands, furthermore, only one of the men had a thin white rope, ready to wrap this around the prince's throat.

The seven men closed in on Mustafa, all of them at once, they jumped on top of him, similar to a soccer match between two teams full of five to six-year-olds, both teams running and jumping at the ball, as ordered by their coaches. The prince was instantly stuck at the bottom of the pile, with seven heavy janissary soldiers on top of him.

Zal Mahmud Pasha, who was among the seven janissary men, and who was wearing black from head to toe, was the janissary that was holding the white rope. Zal Mahmud was trying very hard to position himself behind Mustafa and to place the rope under his chin to pull it, to tighten it, and to strangle him.

We should remember that Zal Mahmud was nicknamed Zal after the legendary hero of the Shahnameh epic poem. Both Zal from the poem and Mahmud were great wrestlers, therefore, the nickname Zal was given to the Ottoman pasha. Hence, Mustafa was not only outnumbered seven to one, but one of the janissary men was a very good wrestler, maybe the best within the borders of the Ottoman Empire.

The odds were not very good. Mustafa had seven men on top of him. He was at the bottom trying to wrestle off, better stated as he was trying to push off these men. While he was at the bottom of the pile of stacked men, he was getting extremely angry. Struck by a rapid increase of anger triggered a reaction in his mind. When Mustafa was subjected to severe emotional stress, especially when against his will, and especially when he was angry, this often lead to him to have a destructive rampage and conflict, which complicated his life, and this was going to be one of those times.

The severe anger and rage he was going through caused a chemical imbalance in his mind, which stopped the flow of oxygen to his head. Plus, the young prince's heart stopped pumping blood to his intellect organ, furthermore, this extreme condition triggered a muscle spasm that only occurred on rare occasions, and as stated above, this was one of those rare occurrences.

Mustafa was still stuck at the bottom of the pile, with seven janissary soldiers on top of him. He stopped struggling and laid still at the bottom of the pile. What was happening? He was growing bigger, literary, he was getting bigger and growing muscles everywhere on his body. Mustafa was growing rapidly, which resulted in his clothes ripping. All his clothes ripped completely off of him, similar to a rattlesnake, shedding the dead skin, nothing was on him, except for his white pants, which were also ripped to resemble as if he was wearing short pants. Moreover, his skin color turned green.

If the esteemed readers are asking, "had Mustafa turned into Hulk?" no, he had not turned into Hulk, He turned into a creature resembling the Hulk, but remember this was the year 1553, not 1962, when the *Incredible Hulk* was first created. This was the Ottoman times, and the creature's name was *Haluk*. At least that was the name given to a monster or creature that was out of this world, during those days in the empire.

The creature named Haluk, which resembled Hulk had no clothes on, only his ripped half pants. Haluk summoned up all his strength and slowly, first, made it up to one knee, then, soon after, made it up to his two feet, standing tall, while all seven janissary men were held high over his head, by his muscular big arms. Zal Mahmud was at the very top of the heap of men. The janissary soldiers were in absolute disbelief and amazed at the current situation, they were not battling the prince, but a green monster, the size of a two-story house.

Haluk had all seven men over his head, then completed three rapid turns, similar to a male ice skater skating gracefully, while holding his female partner over his head and turning. After three rapid full turns, Haluk tossed the seven janissary men into one dark corner of the big make-shift black tent.

The seven janissary men, staggered up on their feet, somewhat slowly, but they made it up to their feet. When they saw Haluk standing at the middle of the tent, bulging with big muscles, green as a lizard, and big as a two-story house, they all ran straight out of the tent, thru the front entrance. Haluk, who was left all alone in the tent and seeing where the exit was, strode calmly out of the black tent as well.

While outside of the front entrance of the make-shift tent, Haluk paused, looked around, and watched as every single janissary soldier that was previously standing around the sultan's tent, ran off into the distant trees, like white-tailed deer running off when they see a big, mean, and stunning grizzly bear.

No one was left standing around the sultan's tent, other than Mustafa, who was momentarily disguised as Haluk.

The above ten short paragraphs did not happen. Sadly, it did not end as written in the above paragraphs. Haluk did not show-up to rescue Mustafa. The sentence-layer was thinking out loud and creating an almost believable new story of Mustafa's super-hero new character. However, it can not be written as such, no.

This did not happen, the young prince did not turn into a green creature and scare away the janissary men, no, that did not happen, unfortunately.

What did happen inside the tent? Mustafa fought a good fight, yes, he did that indeed. But, there were just too many of them. Plus, there was a very strong wrestler among them, the one and only, Zal Mahmud. He, along with the other six janissary men wrestled the **hope** of the people down and kept him down on the ground, until Zal Mahmud was successful in putting the rope under the chin of the prince. Furthermore, he was able to squeeze hard on the thin rope. Mustafa suffocated within a few seconds and stopped breathing. He was dead.

Where was the Lawmaker Sultan Suleiman when the wrestling match was happening? Lawmaker was standing in the second part of the make-shift large tent, watching his eldest son try to wrestle-off seven janissary men. The second part of the tent began behind the baldachin throne seat, where there was a black see-through curtain, this was precisely the spot where the vampire lookalike sultan was standing, watching his son try very hard to not get strangulated.

When Mustafa was finally at the bottom of the pile of men, Lawmaker slowly walked back into the first section of the make-shift black tent and sat on his comfortable throne seat. He sat and watched as his eldest son shook and quivered at the bottom of the pile of men.

As he was watching the lifeless body of his eldest son lie on the ground, after the seven men had gotten off, the Lawmaker was seen to have shed a tear. That is correct, he was sad at seeing his son die, the vampire lookalike sultan had a heart, small heart as it was, he did have one.

What happened next was extraordinary and unbelievable, but it did happen. Zal Mahmud and the other six janissary men, plus Lawmaker Sultan Suleiman were witnesses. The voice of Mustafa was heard bouncing off the black tent walls. His voice was similar to when God spoke with Prophet Moses, from behind a burning acacia bush. The voices of both God and Mustafa were mysterious, divine, and heavenly.

The young prince spoke as follows, *"My sultan father, since you are hearing me speak now, you have executed me and I have passed away from this world, a world full of lies."* Murderer Zal Mahmud and his accomplices, the six janissary men were in complete shock at hearing this voice. They all looked down at the lifeless body of the prince, the lips were not moving, but they were hearing him speak loudly. They did not want to hear his voice speak, therefore, they covered their ears with their hands, while hurriedly running out of the black tent. The only person in the tent was the Lawmaker now. He was still seated, looking up to the sky, better stated, he was looking up at the ceiling of the black tent, praying that his dead son would come back into the tent, come back to life.

Mustafa continued to speak, *"Know this, my sultan father, your hands have my blood on them, and know that you have taken an innocent life. I did not betray you. I swear on my son Mehmet's life, I swear on my two daughters' lives, I did not betray you! Your hands have my innocent blood on them now."*

Lawmaker Sultan Suleiman was seated, and still looking up at the black ceiling yelled out loud, "Mustafam, I was told you betrayed me!"

The voice continued, *"I did not betray you! I am leaving this cruel world, a world where a father kills his son. My name will not be written into the pages of world history, no one will speak of my victories, nor will I have had a throne to preside over. Furthermore, some people will say that I betrayed my father. So be it, let it be written that way. Let them hide the truth, but God knows the full truth. One day, in the future, a day will come, when my story, a story of the oppressed will be told to the people. Maybe that day will come many years from now, or maybe it will come in a few hundred years, but eventually, my story will be told truthfully. The people will hear my story and will learn the truth. And on that day, justice will be given to me, justice will be given to the oppressed."*

Lawmaker Sultan Suleiman was still seated, waited a few seconds, still looking up at the black ceiling. He waited and listened if his son would continue to speak, but that was the end of the voice coming from all corners of the tent. Lawmaker put his head down to look at his palms that were facing up. He whispered regretfully, while tears were rolling down his cheek, "I have the blood of Mustafam, what devil or what fiend did I take advise from..." He did not ask a question, he made a concrete statement to himself as he surely knew who all advised him of the false betrayal activity of Mustafa.

The six elite group of janissary men were outside the sultan's big black tent, and they were waiting for their leader to exit. But instead of seeing their leader come out of the tent, what did they see? They watched in complete surprise as the murderers of Mustafa, the black-wearing janissary men, ran out hurriedly from the big black tent.

The statement *ran out of the tent*, was not entirely accurate. All of the black-wearing janissary men were running out of the tent, except for Zal Mahmud. He was the last man to exit out of the black tent since he had a limp, as he was favoring his left leg. He had injured his leg during the wrestling match with the prince. First time in his wrestling career that Zal Mahmud had injured himself.

All of the black-wearing janissary men kept running, and behind the men was Zal Mahmud, hopping, skipping, limping, and trying to keep up. All of the men kept distancing themselves from the black tent, without looking behind, they only stopped when they felt it was safe to do so, which was the make-shift barrack tents of the janissaries, located 200 meters away.

Mustafa's protection of men, who were startled and alarmed to see the black wearing janissary men hurriedly run out of the sultan's tent, pulled their swords quickly out of their scabbards, all six men pulled their swords out at the same time. The sound of the swords being pulled out at the same time made the sound of a loud thunder strike.

Seeing the young prince's men pull their swords out, the three dozen janissaries that were standing near or close to the entrance of the black tent, and who were more than ready to go off like a pistol that was cocked, did indeed go off, they too pulled their swords out.

The fight between the janissaries began. It was an unfair fight, where the sultan's janissaries massacred the prince's. The sword fight was over very quickly. Red thick blood flood freely in front of the terrible make-shift black tent of Lawmaker Sultan Suleiman.

In the aftermath of the killing, Mustafa's body was left on the same carpet that he laid, inside the terrible and awful black tent for an entire day. The reason the body stayed laid on the carpet for a full day was that the Lawmaker had a very difficult time accepting what had happened.

Lawmaker could not believe that he had given the order to have his eldest son killed, he was heard repeatedly to whisper under his breathe, "what devil or what fiend did I take advice from?"

Another more important difficulty was that the Lawmaker was not convinced that Mustafa was dead, he waited by the dead body, wanting for the young prince to get up from the ground and kiss his hand like he was planning to do when he first entered the black tent. Or, he was waiting for his son to speak again as he did before, but unfortunately for the Lawmaker, nothing happened. Finally, when Lawmaker realized that Mustafa was dead, he was not coming back, or he was not going to talk, Lawmaker, regretfully gave the order to have his son's body placed inside a wooden coffin.

Furthermore, about the same time, Lawmaker was grieving the death of his son, the janissaries heard that Mustafa was murdered and this caused a very big riot in the camp. The janissaries had a meeting among themselves and sent their sergeants to the big black tent to meet the high-ranking officers that were positioned in front of the tent.

The sergeants wanted the body of the young prince, in other words, they demanded the body to be given to them, as they wanted to give him a full sermon by a religious leader. Also, they wanted revenge on the murderers, particularly Grand Vizier

Rustem Pasha, as it was known that the vizier convinced Lawmaker to have Mustafa killed. The seven black-wearing janissaries were just pawns, they knew this and would deal with them separately by beating them silly, breaking a few legs and arms, and sending them to faraway southern hot lands to beat rock.

The high ranking officers relayed the message to the Lawmaker and in return, the Lawmaker informed his janissaries that Rustem was the sole person responsible for the death of Mustafa, and as of today, meaning as of October 7th, Rustem was relieved from his duty as the grand vizier of the empire; he was fired. Upon learning this, the janissaries were content, but they were not happy as their favorite contender for the throne was not alive.

With the order of demotion from the Lawmaker, Rustem boarded a carriage and rode out of the camp, toward the capital city. Eyewitnesses relay that Rustem, who did not come out of his tent, as he was hiding in there, escaped in one piece, gracious to being alive. He waited until most janissaries went to sleep and then sneaked out of his tent, boarded a ready-made carriage at 2:00 a.m. on October 8, and rode off to Istanbul.

The final prayer for Mustafa was held in the afternoon of the same day that Rustem escaped and rode off in, that day being, October 8. It is interesting to note that Mustafa's funeral prayer was the first one to be ever held for a prince or sultan in a janissary camp. Usually, the body of a sultan or a prince that died on the battlefield was sent to the capital city to complete the funeral and burial service. Not for the young prince, the janissary demanded the service be held among them. The janissary army wanted to send Mustafa off like no other, they wanted to send him off to the heavens above as the true sultan of the empire. The chanting of, "Prince Mustafa, our leader our destiny. Prince Mustafa, our leader our destiny. Prince Mustafa, our leader our destiny," did not stop, it lasted for a full hour after the prayer service was completed.

Eyewitnesses relay that Lawmaker Sultan Suleiman was among

the 50,000 plus janissaries attending the funeral service for his son. Furthermore, it is reported that the Lawmaker was also chanting, the words absentmindedly and crying at the same time, "Prince Mustafa, our leader our destiny. Prince Mustafa, our leader our destiny. Prince Mustafa, our leader our destiny."

After the funeral prayer, the body of Mustafa, which was inside the wooden coffin, and the lid of the coffin now being hammered shut was sent to the city of Bursa to be buried at the *Muradiye Complex*. This complex was where most of the relatives of the sultanate family were buried, before Istanbul was conquered.

A second reason why the body was sent to Bursa and not Istanbul was that Lawmaker was advised by his high-ranking officers that there were riots in the capital city upon the news of Mustafa's death. Therefore, it was not advised to send the body to the capital city, since this action would fuel the fire for further riots. It was decided to quietly bury Mustafa's body in Bursa, without too many people knowing where his tomb was.

CHAPTER SEVEN

The conclusion to the sad story

"The residents of the fire cannot be equal to the residents of paradise. Only the residents of paradise will be successful." --- verse 20 from the chapter titled, The exile, of the Quran

"Old and young everyone cries without stopping." --- Taslica Yahya (poem written for Mustafa)

"In this world, there is death, neither you nor I will come out alive.". --- Lyrics from the Turkish song titled, Come to the river, so I can see you, a song by Ufuk Erbas (the writer is unknown)

The recognizable observation about the framework in which Mustafa was executed remained that Lawmaker Sultan Suleiman had lost control of the throne and he was using every means possible to him, to keep his power. In the majority view, Mustafa was superior to his step-brothers in leadership and governance capabilities, and he was even considered preferable to the aging and ill sultan.

It seemed that the Lawmaker was convinced that Mustafa was a threat to his rule. Even if Mustafa never openly rebelled against his father, events positioned him as the potential leader of a rebellion, at least that was how the Lawmaker, his wife Hurrem, their daughter Mihrimah, and their son-in-law Rustem, witnessed the developments.

It seems likely that Suleiman and his close accomplices mentioned above were aware to the possible succession scenarios, including one in which Mustafa, backed by unequivocal military support, could overthrow him. Once overthrown, Mustafa would ascend the throne, and send his father into retirement forever.

Mustafa had gained the favor of the janissaries, scholars, and the common people, who wanted to see him take the throne, even before his sultan father's natural death. If Mustafa had survived to sit on the imperial throne, he would have satisfied a wide spectrum of Ottoman society. The role of social groups in the next sultan's succession to the throne cannot be denied, as they were all involved in the ascension.

The love for Mustafa at the beginning of the decade of 1550's ballooned to the extent that the janissaries disregarded Lawmaker's command when the interests of Mustafa was threatened. Writing in the tale-end of the sixteenth century, historian *Mustafa Bin Ahmet Ali*, described the devotion of the janissary army to Mustafa in such a way that they could defend Mustafa even against the sultan, Ali wrote, "some important men in the army assured me that if Mustafa was able to exit his father's black tent alive, the janissary army would have run to his aid, against his sultan father."

It is strongly believed that if Lawmaker had not acted when he did, as in executed his son, Mustafa would have eventually taken the initiative to dethrone his sultan father, he certainly had the support needed to do so, and the janissaries would have certainly helped him become the next sultan.

However, it did not happen, as in, Mustafa did not try to dethrone his sultan father. He did not initiate any action to take the throne, he chose to wait, which ultimately resulted in him being strangled by the orders of his father.

The death of Mustafa was a tremendously mournful event because he had been loved by the janissaries, bureaucrats, religious scholars, and the common people alike, in short, by almost every influential social group in the empire.

As a result, during the latter part of the year 1553, an atmosphere of tension, panic, and fear was felt in the streets of the capital city. The Topkapi Palace, the home of the sultanate family was repeatedly attacked by people, who were mad and disappointed by the Lawmaker's decision.

Mustafa's execution caused complete upheaval and unrest in all corners of the empire, especially in the districts that he previously governed, these being, Manisa, Amasya, and Konya. The people believed he was going to be the next sultan and when this belief came to an end, with his death, the people were extremely grief-stricken. The people remembered and referred to him years and years after as not Prince Mustafa, but as Sultan Mustafa, even though his life had been cut short, before his rise to the throne. The legend of Mustafa did not subside as the years went by, but only grew larger and larger to become a part of Ottoman literature.

Plus, any person outside of the empire, and who was knowledgeable about the internal affairs of the Ottomans, knew that the number one contender to the throne was killed. This was very sad for them as well, even if they recognized that the death of Mustafa was advantageous for them, as it made the empire weaker.

The commonly accepted story in both major Ottoman historical accounts and the modern scholarly literature was that particularly Hurrem and Rustem cunningly framed Mustafa as a rebel and insurgent in the eyes of the Lawmaker, who ultimately gave the order to execute his innocent eldest son. The Lawmaker was criticized severely for allowing the above-mentioned parties deceive him and for his selfish decisions to preserve his power that ultimately turned the empire from a progressive enterprise into a stagnant and inactive trajectory.

Mustafa Sururi Efendi, who was the personal teacher of Mustafa from the time the prince first came to Istanbul at age five, wrote the following about his pupil, when he heard of the killing, "similar to his sultan father, he was ethical, similar to his grandfather,

Stern Selim, he was gentle and fearless, and similar to his great great grandfather, Conqueror Mehmet, he was smart and intelligent. Mustafa was the brightest prince this mighty empire had ever seen."

After writing the above comparison and comment about Mustafa, the teacher - Mustafa Sururi did not accept any duty from the Lawmaker and never spoke with the sultan again. Mustafa Sururi cut all ties with the Lawmaker and retired in a small house in Istanbul.

The ambassador Monsieur Ogier Ghiselin de Busbecq, wrote the following about Mustafa, once he heard about the killing, "him being the son of a sultan is a great misfortune."

Ottoman historian Mustafa Bin Ahmet Ali, referred to the infamous year of 1553 when Mustafa was executed as the definite moment at which the Ottoman Empire began to decline. The sentence-layer agrees with the historian, and had written in chapter five, the following, "some historians believe that the start of the weakening of the Ottoman Empire, began with Sultan Suleiman since he overextended the resources rather thin. The sentence-layer partially agrees with this point of view, however, believes that the slow weakening did not start during Suleiman's rule, but right after him, during the reign of his son, Sultan Selim II. Troubled times were just around the corner, as Suleiman's latter year policies were not necessarily proper for the empire, and this showed and blossomed during the next regime of the empire."

The poet and companion of Mustafa, Taslica Yahya Bey composed a haunting and tragic elegy, which was written previously in chapter four, however, it is fitting to write it again below:
"Help, help, one side of the world has been devastated,
Angel of death took Sultan Mustafa.

The sun of his beauty set, his council dissolved,
With deceit, they made the family of Ottoman, carry this horrible moment.

They were bad-mouthing him when others mentioned that bravest man,
Fate turned the sultan of the world to their side.

The slander of the lie and his hidden grudge,
Made us shed tears, and lighted the fire of separation.

He didn't murder anyone as they murdered in blood,
He got drowned in the flood of disaster, his men disbanded.

I wish my eyes had not seen this event,
Despaired we were, this judgment was not fit for him.

He got decorated with whites like a minaret lighted at night,
He was genuine like the morning.

He appeared to the people, like a tree in a flower garden,
He walked among his people like a tulip garden.

Sultan of the world was standing with anger, like fire,
His tents were like snowy mountain tops.

They were decorated with bodies like a white fortress,
He walked towards the unstable sun to kiss his hand.

He didn't come back, because he turned into an eclipsed moon,
People who had seen this cried like spring clouds.

This black tent of the world was like a two-headed dragon,
One who falls into the mouth disappears.

That dragon brought the backside of time,
The harm came to his body from the cruelty of Rustem.

The stars of tears were shed, cries increased,
The moment of his death has become a sign of judgment day.

Everywhere has filled with cries, sighs, and tears,
Old and young, everyone cried without stopping.

The tears flooded and flew to the lands,

I wonder if the sultan of the world is on the bed of happiness now?

He, the soul of men became earth,
Is it fair that the evil-doer Satan is alive?

Don't put our sighs on the ground like the evening wind,
They insulted the line of our sultans."

In European drama and literature, the subject of Mustafa's execution had been treated as a tragedy over the years, parallel to the Ottoman sources.

There are multiple examples in Europe about the tragedy of Mustafa, however, only one will be written, since it was the first performance, outside of the borders of the Ottoman Empire.

In the Republic of Venetia, the most popular play performed on stage about the misfortune of Mustafa was titled, *Prospero Bonarelli's Il Solimano*. This play was first performed in the city of *Ancona* in 1618, and is still played in many parts of Italy and the remainder of Europe to this day.

The heartbreak of Mustafa lives on within Turkey, and many other surrounding nations that were once part of the Ottoman Empire. The conversation by the people in these nations become thoughtful and inquisitive when the topic is about the Lawmaker Sultan Suleiman. The sympathetic question is always voiced, what is that question?

"What if Mustafa, the **hope** ascended the throne?"

The question has a couple of scenarios, but the majority can agree and conclude that it would have been better for everyone, especially the Ottoman Empire, if Mustafa ascended the throne in the year of 1553, instead of being executed. But we will never know this fully.

Therefore, this will just be a longing voiced, similar to when a middle aged person, thinks back to their teenager years, to their first love and whispers, "what if I pursued and married my first love?"

The answer will never be known, but the thought and longing continue on.

WORKS CITED

Preface
1. Quote by Yilmaz Guney
https://www.pekguzelsozler.com/yilmaz-guney-sozleri
Chapter One
1. Quote by John Ronald Reuel Tolkien
https://www.goodreads.com/quotes/229-all-that-is-gold-does-not-glitter-not-all-those
2. Quote by Taslica Yahya, poem written for Mustafa
http://www.turkishclass.com/forumTitle_58556
3. Lyrics from the song, Zoo Station, sung by the group named U2 (writers - Adam Clayton, Dave Evans, Larry Mullen, and Paul Hewson
https://songmeanings.com/songs/view/10214/
4. Sehzade Mustafa'ya Ithafen Yazilmis Mersiyeler Siirler (Turkish) (translation) Poems written for Prince Mustafa
http://www.meleklermekani.com/threads/sehzade-mustafaya-ithafen-yazilmis-mersiyeler-siirler.228967/
5. The Rise of the Turks and the Ottoman Empire, by Paul M. Pitman III
6. History of the Turks
http://www.historyworld.net/wrldhis/PlainTextHistories.asp?historyid=aa98
7. Gokturk Empire
http://www.globalsecurity.org/military/world/centralasia/gokturk.htm
8. Transoxania, Historical Region, Asia
https://www.britannica.com/place/Transoxania
9. The Achaemenid Persian Empire (550–330 B.C.)

http://www.metmuseum.org/toah/hd/acha/hd_acha.htm
10. Sasanian Empire
http://www.ancient.eu/Sasanian_Empire/
11. Bukhara
https://www.lonelyplanet.com/uzbekistan/central-uzbekistan/bukhara
12. The Art of the Abbasid Period (750–1258)
http://www.metmuseum.org/toah/hd/abba/hd_abba.htm
13. Sects of Islam
http://www.muslimhope.com/SectsOfIslam.htm
14. Forgotten Hero of Islam: Alp Arslan
https://www.islam21c.com/islamic-thought/forgotten-hero-of-islam-alp-arslan/
15. Anatolia
http://www.allaboutturkey.com/anatolia.htm
16. Rum
https://www.davidmus.dk/en/collections/islamic/dynasties/seljuks-of-rum
17. Romanos IV Diogenes (1068–1071)
http://www.doaks.org/resources/seals/gods-regents-on-earth-a-thousand-years-of-byzantine-imperial-seals/rulers-of-byzantium/bzs.1958.106.600
18. Crusades
https://www.myjewishlearning.com/article/the-crusades/
19. Bithynia
http://www.allaboutturkey.com/bitinya.htm
20. Timur
https://www.thoughtco.com/timur-or-tamerlane-195675
21. Istanbul
https://www.johnsanidopoulos.com/2010/05/different-names-of-constantinople.html
Chapter Two
1. Quote by Sultan Suleiman
http://www.poetrysoup.com/suleiman_the_magnificent
2. Quote by Taslica Yahya
http://www.turkishclass.com/forumTitle_58556

3. Lyrics from the song, Time of the Seasons, sung by the group named Zombies (writer - R. Argent)
https://www.metrolyrics.com/time-of-the-season-lyrics-the-zombies.html
4. Suleiman the Magnificent
http://www.cs.mcgill.ca/~rwest/wikispeedia/wpcd/wp/s/Suleiman_the_Magnificent.htm
5. After 450 Years, archaeologists still hunting for Magnificent Sultan's heart
http://news.nationalgeographic.com/news/2014/06/140620-ottoman-empire-suleyman-hungary-turkey-sultans-heart/
6. Cardinal Richelieu
http://www.historylearningsite.co.uk/france-in-the-seventeenth-century/cardinal-richelieu/
7. Bartolomeo Contarini
https://www.turkcebilgi.com/bartolomeo_contarini
8. Children of Achilles: The Greeks in Asia Minor Since the Days of Troy, by John Freely, pages 175 to 185
https://books.google.ca/books?id=OGzRrs4KkRoC&pg=PA180&lpg=PA180&dq=Bartolomeo+Contarini+suleyman&source=bl&ots=u78rDpHpG8&sig=6SoB5pO8470Y-HtaxGkpC-qz4pQQ&hl=en&sa=X&ved=0ahUKEwiV5JCswuLLAhUG9WMKHTjABB0Q6AEIJzAC#v=onepage&q=Bartolomeo%20Contarini%20suleyman&f=false
9. Suleiman the ruler
http://www.crystalinks.com/suleiman.html
10. The Turkish Letters of Ogier Ghiselin de Busbecq: Imperial Ambassador at Constantinople 1554-1562
http://www.h-net.org/reviews/showrev.php?id=12254
11. Mahidevran explained
http://everything.explained.today/Mahidevran_Sultan/
12. Boutique Ottoman
http://www.boutiqueottoman.com/who-is-hurrem-sultan-roxelana-hoyam-sultana/

13. Roxolana in European Literature, History and Culture, edited by Galina I. Yermolenko, chapter 1 - Roxolana in Europe
https://books.google.ca/books?id=E9DsCwAAQBAJ&pg=PT55&lpg=PT55&dq=gabriel+bounin+la+soltane+english&source=bl&ots=2O5wu8eG7W&sig=Gc_UezHmjKlXH-SWe6Z8ooFWWgnk&hl=en&sa=X&ved=0ahUKEwirtbvX1ezNAhUD1WMKHTSiAWA4ChDoAQgbMAA#v=onepage&q=gabriel%20bounin%20la%20soltane%20english&f=false
14. Muhibbi
https://www.boutiqueottoman.com/suleiman-the-magnificient-muhibbi-a-true-lover/
15. The history of fratricide in the Ottoman Empire - Part 1
https://www.dailysabah.com/feature/2015/08/07/the-history-of-fratricide-in-the-ottoman-empire--part-1

Chapter Three

1. Quote by William Shakespeare
https://www.goodreads.com/work/quotes/1118349-sonnets
2. Quote by Taslica Yahya
http://www.turkishclass.com/forumTitle_58556
3. Lyrics from the song, Midnight, the Stars and You, sung by Ray Noble and his Orchestra, and Al Bowlly (writers - Harry M. Woods, Jimmy Campbell, and Reg Connelly)
https://songbook1.wordpress.com/fx/1930-1939-selected-standards-and-hits/additional-1930s-standards-and-hits/midnight-the-stars-and-you/
4. The Imperial Harem: Women and Sovereignty in the Ottoman Empire, by Leslie P. Peirce, pages 55 to 56
https://books.google.ca/books?id=L6-VRgVzRcUC&pg=PA55&dq=mahidevran&hl=en&sa=X&ved=0ahUKEwj3zaegrL_fAhWGKHwKHWtWDpQQ6AEIKjAA#v=onepage&q=mahidevran&f=false
5. Princess Nazjan Begum
https://www.geni.com/people/Nazan-Begum-Hatun-Giray/6000000028522394599
6. Empress of the East: How a European Slave Girl Became Queen

of the Ottoman, by Leslie Peirce, Chapter: Roxelana's Rival
https://books.google.ca/books?
id=SIuKDgAAQBAJ&pg=PT106&dq=Pietro+Bragadin
+mahidevran&hl=en&sa=X&ved=0ahUKEwj8gtG7rb_fAh-
VmJjQIHaVAB_IQ6AEIMDAB#v=onepage&q=Pietro%20Bragadin
%20mahidevran&f=false
7. Haseki Hurrem
https://www.findagrave.com/memorial/20122003/haseki-
h_rrem
8. Municipal history
https://www.ibb.istanbul/en/SitePage/Index/102
9. Ogier Ghiselin de Busbecq
https://networks.h-net.org/node/15337/reviews/15415/
helfferich-de-busbecq-turkish-letters-ogier-ghiselin-de-busbecq
10. Shah Tahmasp
http://eurasianroyalancestry.com/timeline/shah-tahmasp-i/
11. Why and where did Mustafa die?
https://www.yenicikanlar.com.tr/sehzade-mustafa-neden-ve-
nerede-olduruldu-sehzade-mustafayi-nasil-
katlettiler-09-02-2014-565/
12. The Lawmaker and Prince Mustafa, by Domenico Trevisano,
Bernardo Nabagero
https://www.kobo.com/ca/en/ebook/kanuni-ve-sehzade-
mustafa

Chapter Four

1. Quote by John Fitzgerald Kennedy
https://www.goodreads.com/quotes/89101-those-who-make-
peaceful-revolution-impossible-will-make-violent-revolution
2. Quote by Taslica Yahya
http://www.turkishclass.com/forumTitle_58556
3. Lyrics from the Turkish song titled, Fly away birds (*Ucun kuslar ucun*), song by Ahmet Kaya (writers - Riza Tevfik Bolukbasi and Ahmet Kaya)
http://www.turkuler.com/sozler/
turku_ucun_kuslar_ucun_dogdugum_yere.html
4. Prince Mehmet

https://www.revolvy.com/page/Şehzade-Mehmed

5. Lawmaker Suleiman's fratricide report
https://www.haberturk.com/yazarlar/murat-bardakci/922087-iste-kanuni-suleymanin-evlat-ve-torun-katli-raporu

6. Prince Mehmet Mosque
http://howtoistanbul.com/en/sehzade-mehmet-complex/4785

7. Notable life of Mihrimah Sultan
https://www.dailysabah.com/feature/2014/03/11/notable-life-of-mihrimah-sultan

8. Mihrimah Sultan
https://infogalactic.com/info/Mihrimah_Sultan

9. Son-in-law Rustem Pasa
http://dursunsaral.com.tr/dursunsaral/index.php/2015/11/19/damat-rustem-pasa/

10. The Ottoman Age of Exploration, by Giancarlo Casale, pages 84 to 90
https://books.google.ca/books?id=Xf3h3Z1YQtIC&pg=PA84&dq=rustem+pasha+who&hl=en&sa=X&ved=0ahUKEwidzOrM4PvfAhWICTQIHQPPCqIQ6AEIRDAG#v=onepage&q=rustem%20pasha%20who&f=false

11. Suleiman the Magnificent, by Andre Clot, Chapter 6
https://books.google.ca/books?id=zz0hBQAAQBAJ&pg=PT125&dq=rustem+pasha+who&hl=en&sa=X&ved=0ahUKEwitvZrBiP7fAhXB7oMKHcEjAjk4ChDoAQhCMAU#v=onepage&q=rustem%20pasha%20who&f=false

12. Diplomatic presents
https://books.openedition.org/ifeagd/1652?lang=en

13. Iran Facing Others: Identity Boundaries in a Historical Perspective, by Abbas Amanat, Farzin Vejdani, Chapter 4
https://books.google.ca/books?id=-WJdAQAAQBAJ&pg=PT142&lpg=PT142&dq=prince+bayezid&source=bl&ots=HeffABIyuC&sig=ACfU3U2DZFbxv0jp-mSuXdn2FjcQ7bdQ2MQ&hl=en&sa=X&ved=2ahUKEwjzhpK-m7urtAhXUOn0KHZ0dD8UQ6AEwEnoECB8QAg#v=onepage&q-

=prince%20bayezid&f=false

14. Selim II, Sultan of the Ottoman Empire
https://www.geni.com/people/Selim-II-Sultan-of-the-Ottoman-Empire/6000000008518936710

15. Sultan 'Selim the Drunkard', who initiated the downfall of the Ottoman Empire
https://lordsofthedrinks.com/2014/12/21/sultan-selim-ii-the-drunkard-who-initiated-the-downfall-of-the-ottoman-empire/

16. Turkish and Islamic Art Museum: The Palace of Grand Vizier Ibrahim Pasha
http://www.turkishneurosurgery.org.tr/pdf/pdf_JTN_1384.pdf

17. Restoring the executioner's mosque
https://www.hurriyetdailynews.com/restoring-the-executioners-mosque-18937

18. The killing that upset everyone, Mustafa, the sultan in everyone's heart
https://onedio.com/haber/idami-herkesi-yasa-bogan-osmanli-nin-tahtsiz-padisahi-sultan-mustafa--599130

19. Taslıcalı Yahya: A janissary poet
https://www.dailysabah.com/portrait/2017/04/15/taslicali-yahya-a-janissary-poet

20. A Janissary Poet: Yahya of Taslica
http://www.raillife.com.tr/en/a-janissary-poet-yahya-of-taslica/

Chapter Five

1. Quote by Malcolm X
https://www.goodreads.com/quotes/tag/betrayal

2. Quote by Taslica Yahya
http://www.turkishclass.com/forumTitle_58556

3. Lyrics from the Turkish song titled, Just love me back (*Sev yeter*), song by Muslum Gurses (writers - Ali Tekinture and Ugur Bayar)
https://www.sarkisozleri.bbs.tr/sarki/6479/sev-yeter

4. Prince mosque
https://www.weloveist.com/listing/sehzade-mosque

5. Prince Mustafa
https://peoplepill.com/people/sehzade-mustafa/

6. The Sulaiman-nama (Suleiman-name) as an Historical Source,

by Fatma Sinem Eryılmaz, pages: 165 to 180
https://brill.com/view/book/edcoll/9789004356252/
BP000019.xml
7. Medieval Sourcebook: The Legends & Poetry of The Turks, selections
https://sourcebooks.fordham.edu/source/turkishpoetry1.asp
8. Muradiye Mosque & Tombs, Bursa
https://turkeytravelplanner.com/go/ThraceMarmara/bursa/
sights/muradiye.html
9. Mustafa Mukhlisi (1515-1553)
https://www.turquie-culture.fr/pages/lettres-turques/
biographies/mustafa-mukhlisi-le-prince-poete-assassine.html
10. August 6 Zodiac is Leo - Full Horoscope Personality
https://www.thehoroscope.co/zodiac-signs/august-6-zodiac-
leo.html
11. Secrets of Istanbul
https://www.istanbulunsirlari.net/once-vefa-diyen-bir-alim-
sururi-mustafa-efendi/
12. Rustem Pasha
https://ottoman.ahya.net/node/122
13. Rustem Pasa
https://islamansiklopedisi.org.tr/rustem-pasa
Chapter Six
1. Quote by Benjamin Franklin
https://www.goodreads.com/author/
quotes/289513.Benjamin_Franklin
2. Quote by Taslica Yahya
http://www.turkishclass.com/forumTitle_58556
3. Lyrics from the rap song, Fear of a black planet, by the group,
Public Enemy (writer - Chuck D.)
http://www.rapquote.com/tag/public-enemy/
4. Suleiman The Magnificent
https://historycollection.com/12-rulers-executed-relatives/5/
5. Hurrem Sultan: A beloved wife or master manipulator?
https://www.dailysabah.com/feature/2015/01/09/hurrem-
sultan-a-beloved-wife-or-master-manipulator

6. Medieval Sourcebook: The Legends & Poetry of The Turks, selections
https://sourcebooks.fordham.edu/source/turkishpoetry1.asp
7. The killing that upset everyone, Mustafa, the sultan in everyone's heart
https://onedio.com/haber/idami-herkesi-yasa-bogan-osmanli-nin-tahtsiz-padisahi-sultan-mustafa--599130
8. Son-in-law Rustem Pasa
http://dursunsaral.com.tr/dursunsaral/index.php/2015/11/19/damat-rustem-pasa/
9. The religious leader during Lawmaker's time, Ebussuud Efendi
http://www.istanbultarih.com/kanuni-devri-nin-seyhulislami-ebussuud-efendi-274.html
10. The religious leader Ebu Suud's answer to Sultan Suleiman
https://www.aksam.com.tr/televizyon/seyhulislam-ebu-suud-efendinin-sultan-suleymana-cevabi/haber-282523
11. Superhero Science: The Hulk
http://www.planet-science.com/categories/over-11s/human-body/2012/04/superhero-science-the-hulk.aspx
12. What type of plant was the bush of Exodus 3:2?
https://hermeneutics.stackexchange.com/questions/15609/what-type-of-plant-was-the-bush-of-exodus-32

Chapter Seven
1. Verse 20 from the chapter titled, The exile, of the Quran
https://quran.com/59
2. Quote by Taslica Yahya
http://www.turkishclass.com/forumTitle_58556
3. Lyrics from the Turkish song titled, Come to the river, so I can see you (*Pinara gelki gorem*), song by Ufuk Erbas (writer is unknown)
https://turkusozu.net/pinara-gel-ki-gorem/
4. Mustafa Muslihuddin Sururi
https://islamansiklopedisi.org.tr/sururi-muslihuddin-mustafa
5. The Turkish Letters of Ogier Ghiselin de Busbecq, Imperial Ambassador at Constantinople, by Edward Seymour Forster
https://www.jstor.org/stable/25221464?seq=1

6. Bureaucrat and intellectual in the Ottoman Empire: the historian Mustafa Ali (1541-1600, by Cornell H. Fleischer

Cover Art

A drawing of a tulip.

About the Author

Ridvan Akbay grew up in Istanbul, Turkey, but lived part of his life in Canada. He is the author of the books, THE DEVOTED CALL FOR HOPE, BLACK TENT, MOTHER TO A PRINCE, THE GOLD BRACELET, VISIT FROM AN ANGEL, THE PROUD STAND, and THE OBSESSION, published by Ben Oak Publishing via Amazon Kindle Direct Publishing.

Made in the USA
Middletown, DE
20 June 2021